FROM CO DURHAM

Edited by Allison Dowse

First published in Great Britain in 2000 by
YOUNG WRITERS
Remus House,
Coltsfoot Drive,
Woodston,
Peterborough, PE2 9JX
Telephone (01733) 890066

All Rights Reserved

Copyright Contributors 1999

HB ISBN 0 75431 767 6
SB ISBN 0 75431 768 4

FOREWORD

This year, the Young Writers' Future Voices competition proudly presents a showcase of the best poetic talent from over 42,000 up-and-coming writers nationwide.

Successful in continuing our aim of promoting writing and creativity in children, our regional anthologies give a vivid insight into the thoughts, emotions and experiences of today's younger generation, displaying their inventive writing in its originality.

The thought, effort, imagination and hard work put into each poem impressed us all and again the task of editing proved challenging due to the quality of entries received, but was nevertheless enjoyable. We hope you are as pleased as we are with the final selection and that you continue to enjoy *Future Voices From Co Durham* for many years to come.

CONTENTS

Belmont Comprehensive School
Laura Smith	1
Philip J Simpson	2
Stacey Houldsworth	2
Jennifer Weir	3
Sarah Louise Dawson	4
Ian Portsmouth	4
Laura Platten	5
Casey Rees	5
Ashleigh Crampton	6
Louise Turnbull	7
Kathryn Thompson	8
Michael Dodds	8
Anne Venner	9
Catherine Herbert	10
Katie Holmes	10
Michael Burrows	11
Alison Peachey	12
Jack Errington	12
Daryl Scott	13
Daniel Clark	14
Simon Laws	15
Beth Smurthwaite	16
Elizabeth Venner	17

Carmel Technology College
Jonathan De Wind	18
Kayleigh Metcalfe	18
James Flanagan	19
Sarah Rayner	20
Toni Kerrault	20
Sinéad Carla Bogle	21
Robert Creighton	21
Victoria Trodden	22
Lydia Fae Hardy	22

Eleanor Naseby	23
Adam Brown	24
Matthew Thompson	24
Natalie Crowley	25
David Suleiman	26
Charlotte Robinson	26
Lisa Chou	27
Sarah Anne Fawcett	27
Richard Blaylock	28
Thomas Anderson	28
Emma Hall	29
Helen Porter	29
Vicky Dalton	30
Cathy Harris	30
Stuart Cameron	31
Kayley Hunter	32
Rebecca Clarke	32
Sophie Heywood	33
Daniel Hanratty	34
Joel Alderson	35
Laura Fawcett	36
Francesca Denham	37
Catherine Benson	37
Amy Flanagan	38
Rebecca White	38
Carrianne Green	39
Duncan Harrison	40
Lucy Cooper	40
Philip Buxton	41
Ruth Maddison	42
Rachael Taylor	43
Samantha Winchester	43
Stacey Young	44
Sophie-Jo Quick	44
Thomas Pattison	45
Laura McEvoy	46
Philip Jones	46

Kashya Caplice	47
Kayley Smith	48
Katrina Busby	48
Josie Grierson	49
Hannah Ramsey	50
Liam Russell	50
Gemma Walker	51
Claire Ward	51
Jamie Wicks	52
Rachel Louise Murdoch	52
Thomas Reeves	53
Beth Blake	53
Louise Barras	53
Daniel Hall	54
Adam Grieve	54
Thomas Eldrington	55
Jenny Bell	55
Claire Richardson	56
Catherine McKeown	56
Christopher McGovern	57
Stuart Brennan	57
Michelle Tsang	58
Andrew McElvaney	58
Nadia Piper	59
Charlotte Oldham	59
Danielle Hossell	60
William Barras	60
Sarah Hullah	61
Sophie Knapton	61
Jenny Redmond	62
Elinor Campbell	62
Lisa McCallion	63
Stuart Luff	63
Karma McElvanna	64
Leanne Rolfe	64
Callum Rose	64
Catherine Stokell	65

Alec Bowman	65
Joanna Reed	66
Sam Ferguson	66
Jason McSherry	67
Sophie Boyle	67
Joanne Charlton	68
Oliver Harker	68
Sarah Hancocks	69
Alexander Hardy	69
Andrew Hickson	70
Rachel Cassidy	70
Michael Rumfitt	71
Marc Smith	71
Matthew Pease	72
Saskia van Vlijmen	72
Laura Wake	73
David Cornforth	74
Andrew McKenzie	75
Jonathan Gunnell	76
Vicky Warden	76
Catherine Harrison	77
Alan Barr	77
Lizzie Jones	78
Ruth McGuckin	79
Becky Lane	79
Samantha Barker	80
Rory Grierson	80
Philip McDonald	81
Samuel Foster	81
Sophie Weddell	82
Daniel Hustwick	83
Rebecca Wright	83
Patrick Wake	84
Lisa Hall	84
Daniel Robson	85
Gillian McGuigan	85
Josie Miller	86

Emma Rowlinson	86
Aimee Campion	87
Rachel Armstrong	88
Rachel Baker	89
Felicity Cooper	90
Leanne Knight	90
Natalie Boyle	91
Michael Brennan	92
Terrianne Hauxwell	92
Hannah Carr	93
Michael Hayman	94
Elizabeth Smyth	94
Claire Wilson	95
Anthony Savage	96
Jennifer Morgan	97
Elizabeth Steel	98
Michael Collins	99
Donna Varley	100
Gary Johnson	100
Emily MacGregor	101
Danielle Stott	102
Kaylee Scaife	103
Sarah Smith	104

Easington Community School

Danielle Cammock	105
Helen Alp	105
Nikki Foster	106
Helen Smith	107
Jennifer Styles	108
Vicky Maddison	109
Kirsty Golden	110
Donna Weatherall	111
Elizabeth Long	112
Stephanie Armstrong	113
Deborah Milburn	114
Gemma Hough	115

Samantha Richardson	116
Kayleigh Rawlinson	116
Chloe Shaw	117
Ashley Hutton	118
Faye Boyle	119
Janine Colwill	120
Kym Nugent	121
Dale Roberts	122
Faye Thompson	123
Karen Bainbridge	124
Karl Davis	125

Fyndoune Community College

Michael Lee	125
Paul Rowland	126

Greenfield Comprehensive School

Deborah Jewell	126
Sabrina Parker	127
Shannon Peacock	128
Lynsey Bailey	128
Craig Taylor	129
Anna Drury	130
Claire Brown	130
Emma-Jane Robinson	131
Lisa Robinson	131
Kayleigh Harle	132
Victoria Wilson	132
Katy Miller	133
Lucy Bradley	134
Andrew Richardson	135
Catherine Bell	135

Hurworth Comprehensive School

Donna Austin	136
Stephen Tremewan	136
Kelly Pybus	137

Jonathan Roche	137
Alison Galpin	138
William John Harrison	138
Emma Graham	139
Evan Smith	139
Toni Elizabeth Leach	140
Samantha Oates	140
Lauren Robinson	141
Steven Wilson	141
Nichola Ingledew	142
Cally Jameson	142
Kayleigh Evans	143
Laura Bernstone	143
Jennie Haines	144
Michael Lawson	144
Katy Williamson	145
Tanya Atkinson	145
Laura Todd	146
Hayley Waters	146
Laura Evans	147
Sarah Newrick	148
Peter Hedley	148
Danielle Ratti	149
Fern Holmes	150
Katherine Hodgson	151
James Humphreys	151
Daniel Robinson	152
Stuart Lowis	152
Oliver Welch	153
Andrew Bernstone	154
Jennifer Tremewan	155
David Parsons	156
Harry Knott	156
Rachael Doubleday	157
Jonathan Dees	158
Gemma Coverdale	159
Chris Devlin	160

Sarah June Johnston	160
Andrew Leighton	161
Alex Moore	162
Daniel McDowell	163
Gemma Phillips	164
Sara Allan	164
Lee Weeks	165
Shahnaz Romeela Rana-Rahman	166
Sacha Marie Buckley	167
Claire Reese	168
Emma Todd	169
Sophie Oldridge	170
Gemma Wilson	170
Nicola Foster	171
Rozi Smith	172
James Chapman	173
Amy Sedgwick	174

Hurworth House School

Nokkaew Harrington	174
Daniel P Hall	175
Stephen Looney	175
Ben Harrison	176
John Harland	176
Ramesh Pani	177
Fergus Dent	177
Anthony Scott	178
Alex Strachan	178
Guy Severs	179
Alexander Gardner	179
David Burningham	180
Scott Prior	180

Moorside Community School

Joanne Smith	181
Claire Tilney	181
Philip Stephenson	182

Liam Galloway	182
Mark Turner	183
Kimberley Kirsopp	184
Shauna Haley	185
Katie Little	186
Marc Gaines	187
Andrew Williamson	188
David Brewis	188
Laura Kennyford	189
Laura Brown & Laura Collingwood	190
Pamela Butterfield	191
Laura Bean	192
Victoria Bottle	193
Janine Collins	194
Nicola Price	195
Louise Kay	195
Richard Chapman	196
Katie Lloyd	196
Kieran Sharp	197
Donna Matthews	197
Richard Roe	198
Ritchie Rackham	199
Richard Walford	199
Caroline Slater	200
Helen Erving	200
Richard Flowers	201
Kim Brown	202
Benjamin Gibson	202
Paul Heatherington	203
Gemma Symonds	204
Stacey Bell	205

St John's School, Bishop Auckland

Sean Kay	205
Richard Morley	206
Katy Graham	207
Simon Temby	208

Penny Foster	209
Michael Kirtley	210
Rebecca Ferry	211
Casey Mangles	212
Carl McGregor	213
Sara Elmes	214
Emma Haley	215
Michael Hartmann	216
Robert Jones	217
Mark Henry	218
Philip Santana Smith	219
Emma Barker	220

The Poems

THE FUTURE'S FEELINGS

Look to the future,
What do you see?
I see a man in a mask,
Who is waiting for thee.
Does the man in the mask
Look friend or foe?
Please do not ask that
For that I don't know
Personality is something not seen
It can cause discomfort if you know
What I mean.
Oh please forgive me,
But please answer one more
Does this man feel afraid, or
Does this man feel scared in
Any way?
Now, once again, this I can't say.
For feelings are beyond all that
I can see,
They hide deep inside you,
A bit like me.
I hide inside your head,
Yes, I'm not alive,
The future's for no one to see
It comes gliding by.

Laura Smith (11)
Belmont Comprehensive School

A Winter's Night

On a cold winter's night
Walking into a blizzard
After a hard day at school
Crunching through the snow
Looking forward to sitting next to a roaring fire
On a cold winter's night

On a cold winter's night
An icy wind blows
Over the frosty ground
Freezing the fallen leaves
Looking forward to a steaming mug of cocoa
On a cold winter's night

On a cold winter's night
The flakes of snow fall
Onto the frozen pavement
Covering all the roofs
Looking forward to a day of sledging
On a cold winter's night.

Philip J Simpson (11)
Belmont Comprehensive School

A Hallowe'en Night!

As the witches fly on their brooms,
The children dress up in their rooms.
As vampires, witches and bats,
While listening to the scream of the cat.

I cover my face in paint,
To be sure I'll make someone faint.
Dressed up as a hideous ghoul,
I'll frighten my friends from school.

My pumpkin's flickery light,
Will scare some people tonight.
As I knock on the door and hope for a sweet,
The first words I say will be *'Trick or treat?'*

Stacey Houldsworth (11)
Belmont Comprehensive School

SOS!

The blue whale, the manatee,
The bald eagle, the chimpanzee,
How will our animals survive?
The sea turtle, the playful dolphin,
The tiger, the snapping terrapin,
How can we keep them alive?

The hippo, the horned narwhal,
The African elephant, the seagull,
Why should we stand by?
The lion, the wriggly snake,
The cheetah, the swimming drake,
Why should we see them die?

S o innocent and hard to replace,
O ur help is their saving grace,
S o please listen and take heed,

S ome extinct now; others in need,
O nly a minority of some remain,
S o help is needed that is plain.

Jennifer Weir (11)
Belmont Comprehensive School

MY FIRST DAY BACK AT SCHOOL

My first day back at school,
Mam and Dad, smiling,
Shoes shine on children's feet,
Children, looking smart and neat.

Hope in their faces,
Chairs scraping across the floor,
They are hoping for something
to eat,
As they walk into the dinner
hall.

Pens and pencils given out,
New tables shine,
Up the curtain rises,
On the same old stage!

Sarah Louise Dawson (11)
Belmont Comprehensive School

THE FUTURE AND MYSELF

The future is near
The future is clear
I can't wait to be there
I'm only eleven.
Things have changed
Since I was seven
An astronaut I could be!
Flying cars and virtual pets
Are things that there could be.
In the future I hope there will be
A peaceful place for all to see.

Ian Portsmouth (11)
Belmont Comprehensive School

GRANDAD

Grandad, what's it like in heaven?
Is it nice and is everything white?
Do you have your own cloud and halo,
Or is it just sky with a few clouds?

Everyone misses you down here,
We know you're never coming back,
But you'll always be in our hearts,
Even though you're gone.

The millennium is going to be
Really big,
It's a shame you can't celebrate
It with us.
It won't be the same
But we'll think of you all the
Way through.

Laura Platten (11)
Belmont Comprehensive School

MILLENNIUM

Now it's 1999,
Soon it will be time,
For the year 2000 is near,
The new millennium is becoming clear,
New inventions we will see,
I wonder what they will be,
I can't wait for it to come,
The year 2000, the millennium.

Casey Rees (11)
Belmont Comprehensive School

THE FUTURE

I look into the future
And what do I see?
Wedding bells ringing
For whom will it be?

I think of an occupation
What will I be?
Will I be a teacher
Or work under the sea?

I think of my home
And where I will be
Living in England
Or maybe Bali?

I think of future travelling
How will it be?
By space shuttle to the moon
Being home in time for tea?

I think of technology
How will it be?
Computers doing everything
Don't you agree?

I think of my life
How will it be?
Will I be famous
Or just simply me?

I think of the future,
But no one can see,
What they will be doing,
Or who holds the key!

Ashleigh Crampton (11)
Belmont Comprehensive School

HALLOWE'EN

When Hallowe'en comes around,
You will hear on the ground,
Noises of pattering feet,
Little children you're sure to meet.

Open your door during the night,
Children jump out and give you a fright,
'Trick or treat' you hear them scream,
Sweets appear and their faces beam.

Scary witches and ghastly ghouls,
It's only children playing fools,
Just out to have a little fun,
Before the Hallowe'en night is done.

Bobbed for apples, their hair's now wet,
Face paint's all runny, but no one's upset,
For everyone's had a wonderful time,
But now the clocks are beginning to chime.

Abandoned pumpkins light the way,
The night is soon becoming day,
All fast asleep now in their beds,
The ghosts and witches rest their heads.

Louise Turnbull (11)
Belmont Comprehensive School

OUR FUTURE

The future is in our hands
we choose our future.
What we do, who we see
it's up to us.
We are in charge of our planet.
We are in charge of our future.
If we choose to destroy it, it's our choice.
If we destroy it we destroy our homes.
If our planet dies we die with it.
We can have a good future and a good life.
This will only happen if we take care of our planet.
This will only happen if we pick litter up
and walk short distances.
Little things like this will save our planet.
Save our future.
Little things like this will save our lives.

Kathryn Thompson (14)
Belmont Comprehensive School

FUTURE VOICES

Some people say that the future is here now,
But how can the future be here right now?
Great leaps forward in technology and science,
Are still to come to the home appliance.

In 1969 man landed on the moon,
So, hopefully, man will land on Mars very soon,
Cars now drive around on wheels without a bother,
But soon they will probably hover.

Our world it seems will be overcrowded,
We won't let our future horizons be clouded,
Man will achieve as only man dare,
We will have space cities in the air.

Michael Dodds (13)
Belmont Comprehensive School

MILLENNIUM CELEBRATIONS (OR NOT?)

Millennium
Y2K, year two thousand
Subject on everyone's minds.

Wait! Scrape the surface off this cover
What is it?
Another year? Hope that there's some luck in it for me.

Massive celebrations, entertaining and pleasing the world
Drinking, music, dancing and singing
Seeing the new millennium through.

Ten months time
Will two thousand years make difference or change?
Or will all we recall be the wild parties and merrymaking
On that certain New Year's Eve?

Will we remember the war, the hard times or the pain?
Or will all we think of be some insignificant person's fame?
So what's so important about the Y2K?
Isn't it just a cliché?

Anne Venner (13)
Belmont Comprehensive School

LOOKING FORWARD INTO THE FUTURE

In the future . . .
Land mines, bombs and guns
I think all should be banned.
And it's up to us to give it a
bit of a helping hand.
Let's try and make it happen
then we will all be laughing!
In the future . . .
Will we all wear spacesuits
or a pair of cardboard boots?
Space is the final frontier
but in the year 2000 will we
all still be living here?

Catherine Herbert (13)
Belmont Comprehensive School

THE DAY NO ONE WILL FORGET

Will the sky be still blue, with clouds that are white?
Will the leaves fall off the trees when it's autumn?
Will the clocks stop?
Will we have to use candles to see through the darkness?
Will the computers crash?
Will the country grind to a halt?
Will we survive the Millennium Bug?

Will alarms ring?
Will bells sound out?
Will people run out of their houses and shout?
Will we survive the Millennium Bug?

Katie Holmes (11)
Belmont Comprehensive School

THE FUTURE

In the future there will be many changes
There won't be Porsches or any Rangers
Flying cars and household robots
Or even yummy chocolate doughnuts.

But we decide our own future
Whether it's good or whether it's bad
Or even if it's very sad.

With war and hunger in today's life
Who knows what the future will be like
Laser guns and powerful bombs
Everybody is doing everything wrong.

But if we don't fight and get on well
The whole world will not be in hell
And we can set our future to be
What we all would love it to be.

Robots doing all the ironing
And all the washing too
While we relax and watch TV
And see . . . Newcastle win the Premiership!

Well in the future there will be miracles too
You know.

Michael Burrows (13)
Belmont Comprehensive School

CHRISTMAS TO THE MILLENNIUM

Snow is falling all around,
a cold, white blanket covers the ground.
A shiny, white cobweb on the window ledge,
the turkey is cooking and so is the veg.
Tearing away paper,
it's flying everywhere.
What is inside?
You handle with great care.
Darkness has fallen,
but the fun doesn't end here,
the millennium's to come,
so let's grab a beer.
Dancing all night,
until daylight has come,
grab some leftover pud to fill up your tum.
Then back to bed to hear a call,
'Mum, it's still snowing, here's a snowball!'

Alison Peachey (13)
Belmont Comprehensive School

IN THE FUTURE

In the future I want to be able to fly to Mars,
In the future we should have flying cars.

In the future robots should do the housework,
In the future Britain shouldn't be ruled by a jerk.

In the future people shouldn't get too drunk,
In the future people's fortunes may have shrunk.

In the future it's your call what you do,
In the future you can change your friends if you want to.

In the future if you want something, go out and fight,
In the future if you want something, it won't matter if
                                                you're black or white.

In the future we should be friends forever,
In the future, if we want to achieve these things we need
                                                to work together.

Jack Errington (13)
Belmont Comprehensive School

THE FUTURE OF HOME

The home is a simple thing
Which we all take for granted.
Doors are rectangular, windows square,
The roofs are mainly slanted.
What's around the corner? No one knows, not us.
A hoverboard, the flying car or even a floating bus.
So back to the home we go, but what's in store for us?
Talking toaster, tattie roaster, the clever coffee cup?
A mop and bucket I wish, I wish,
That simply tidies up?
Robotic blinds, motorised mat, the electronic cat?
Metallic dog to fetch your post, to chew your glove and hat?
But there are some things I hope won't change
In the bright and cheery future,
That's Mum and Dad and all that jazz
Cos they're a whiz,
Just like my computer!

Daryl Scott (13)
Belmont Comprehensive School

THE WORLD'S FUTURE

The world will change by . . .

People will live on the moon
with cars and space stations,

Computers will do all the jobs
that we try hard on, until
now the computer does it for us,

Cars will fly and change
to a new power,

We will be able to travel to space
for our holiday on a space shuttle,

We will be able to go through
other galaxies with
new spacecrafts,

The world will have peace
and work together
on new technology,

The world will be full
of technology,
we see what will happen
in the future . . .

Daniel Clark (14)
Belmont Comprehensive School

WRESTLING

As the wrestlers enter,
The music starts to play,
Out comes Mankind,
To a shatter and a crash.

Out comes Rocko and Socko,
On Mankind's hand,
As he walks towards the ring,
The crowd begins to sing.

He slides into the brightly lit ring,
The crowd is all around,
He raises Mr Rocko,
Then raises Mr Socko.

He lowers them down,
As Triple H comes down,
Into the very same ring,
And then the bell went 'ding,'

Triple H charged towards him,
Only to be hit,
Picked up and body slammed,
DDT and suplex.

Down to the floor with a
Double arm DDT,
Followed by the Mandible Claw.
Triple H submitted.

'Ding' went the bell again,
Up stood Mankind with belt in his hand,
He was the champion
Of the whole wide world.

Simon Laws (14)
Belmont Comprehensive School

FUTURE VISIONS

The millennium
What does it really mean?
The end of all hope?
The start of a dream?

Who knows what will happen
When Big Ben hits midnight
Will darkness fall eternally
Or will there forever be light?

Nobody knows for sure.
But one thing I know
Is that no matter where I am
Anxiety will show.

I want the millennium
To bring something great.
Love, peace and happiness,
Not war or hate.

So will we be happy
Or will we be sad?
Is the new millennium
Going to be so bad?

Well, there really is only one way to find out.
And although it may sound rash,
Let's just hope that on January 1st
It is only fireworks which flash.

Beth Smurthwaite (13)
Belmont Comprehensive School

I Look, I Search, I See

My eyes look into the distance,
As far away as they can see.
Searching for the past remains
Of remnants of history.

But the more I strain my eyes,
And listen hard for the faintest sound,
The more the truth and lies are mixed,
More vague is the truth already found.

Yes, there are facts which will blare out loud.
They will stay the same.
For who'd invent the invasions, the wars,
The treachery, cowardice and shame?

Yet the past was not all terrible times,
Just think of heroic deeds done.
And what about those who've invented things,
And made life for us more fun?

My eye wanders back to the present stage,
But still, things are not as they should be.
The wars are as bad, the environment worse,
Animals are no longer free.

On the other hand people are healthier now.
Life is much more pleasant.
On the whole, I think there are a lot of things
Which can be said for the present.

I look ahead to the future now,
The present takes leave and goes.
What will happen in years to come?
Only the future knows . . .

Elizabeth Venner (13)
Belmont Comprehensive School

PREDATORS

Super alien race, consuming all the distant solar system
with their alien spawn, creatures looking like hulking humanoid
warriors, some as big as eight feet tall.
Some have spikes here and there
with old, lank, black, dusty and beaded hair,
with their funny coloured skin covered in black and yellow spots.

The thing they do best with the most skill is hunt,
when they find their prey they jump, scream and grunt.
With a few swift moves they decapitate and disembowel
the unfortunate victim, in the style of a Samurai.
Polished and clean with a shine,
the skull acts as a trophy on a shrine.

They travel in organically made space ships,
shooting off like comets at the speed of light.
Able to menace and destroy planets and life
wherever they choose.
They come and go as they please,
don't mess with them or they'll mess with you.

Jonathan De Wind (12)
Carmel Technology College

THE COUNTRYSIDE

Walking through the countryside
Makes my body feel alive
Catching the sun flickering through the trees
Watching leaves fall with a gentle breeze.

Far in the distance I see a pond
Scattered with dazzling white swans
As the sun shines down on gleaming grass
Lots of little birds fly past.

Listening to all the different sounds
That I hear all around
As the trees are rustling, the bees are buzzing
And the birds just happily sing.

Kayleigh Metcalfe (12)
Carmel Technology College

MILLENNIUM

The end is nigh
and spirits are high,
fireworks and bangers,
parties and banners.

Junk food and soft drinks,
balloons and hop skips,
happiness and laughter,
bob sleigh rides after.

The Millennium Dome,
the Millennium Wheel,
will it work,
or will it keel?

The year 2000,
the Millennium Bug,
a new year dawns,
enjoy the fun!

Well whatever you do enjoy it,
you will only see it once,
the past and the present,
will never be rerun.

James Flanagan (12)
Carmel Technology College

GREEN

Green is the colour of
Peter Pan's suit.
Green is the colour of
my lava lamp.
Green is the colour of the
stem that will grow through the summer.
Green is the colour of the
witch's tongue.
Green is the colour of
a chocolate mint cream.
Green is the colour of the
leaves on the trees
Green is the colour of seaweed.
Green is the colour of the traffic
light that makes the cars go.
Green is my favourite.

Sarah Rayner (12)
Carmel Technology College

RED

Furious, enraged, angry red
Hot, stinging, steaming red
'Stop, stop, stop' says red
Siren sounds are red
Holly berries on a tree
Rosy apples and an angry tree
Red leaves that in autumn fall
Red is the best colour of all.

Toni Kerrault (12)
Carmel Technology College

AUTUMN TO WINTER

Now the summer has faded away,
the life of autumn to winter begins.
With leaves that fall like crinkly crisps
from the wintry blue sky.
Children are running like the wind with their
faces as red as roses and lit with joy.
Autumn's crystal-clear rain leads into the
soft, snowy, wintry days.
Soon the loud streets are quiet, everything is
silver silent, no one is out to play.
Christmas lights are here, bells ring,
snow falls, people sing.
That's autumn to winter.

Sinéad Carla Bogle (13)
Carmel Technology College

GREEN

Green is the grass glistening in the sun.
It is a sweet grape in a fruit basket.
Green is for *go, go, go* on a traffic light.
It is a crocodile paddling through the river.
Green is the colour for nature
And a wet, slippery snake slithering through
the long grass.
Green are the trees' arms swaying in the wind.
It is a pea rolling around and around
on an empty plate.
Green is a juicy apple for someone's healthy dinner.
Green is the colour of jealousy.

Robert Creighton (12)
Carmel Technology College

THE FORBIDDEN CASTLE

I'm lost in the woods,
My horse ran away,
It's cold, it's dark,
There's nowhere to stay.
I see a castle up on a cliff,
It's gloomy, it's dark,
I suppose it's okay.
I walk straight in,
I hear a noise,
There're clocks and pans that look like toys.
A beast runs down and grabs my hand,
I'm thrown in a dungeon, where I stand.
I hear him roar every day,
I need to get out, is there a way?

Victoria Trodden (13)
Carmel Technology College

WHAT WOULD LIFE BE LIKE ON THE MOON?

What would life be like on the moon?
Maybe we'll find out some day soon.
What will we have to call our home?
A crater under a huge glass dome.
What will we eat while we're up in space?
Moon food of course, that's what we'll get
While up in that place.
Vacuum packed this and vacuum packed that
You could fit a week's meals into a hat!
What will life be like on the moon?
One day we'll find out, one day soon.

Lydia Fae Hardy (12)
Carmel Technology College

THE STATUE

Who lives in that house? Who could it be?
My curiosity got the better of me.
I was looking so hard that I couldn't see,
The shadows that were following me.

A statue whispered from behind a bush,
'If you go in there you'll die from the crush.'
The finger-like branches said 'Rush girl, rush,'
But I could hear no noise for all of the hush.

I opened the door and entered the house,
I immediately stepped on a large woodlouse.
Cases of animals, the hall littered with grouse,
But in I crept as quiet as a mouse.

The air was heavy with a musty stench,
There was a scratching noise from behind a bench.
Something grabbed me, I drew back with a wrench,
I kept on walking, my fists in a clench.

I ran to the door, turned the handle with a squeak,
It wouldn't open, just gave a loud creak.
Suddenly the hall began to wreak,
I fell to the floor, feeling terribly weak.

My head was spinning, I was passing out,
I had no strength to scream or shout.
The wall's coming in, there was no way out,
All I could do was sit and count.

And now I wait, a lonely statue,
To warn people like me or you,
There's danger in there, if only you knew,
It's happened before, it could happened to you.

Eleanor Naseby (13)
Carmel Technology College

THE MAN WITHOUT A BRAIN

There's a house down Surrey Lane,
Where a man lives that has no brain.
This man has a horse's mane,
He sleeps on a bed where there is a lot of rain.

He works in the shop at the back of the house,
Where he keeps a grouse and a little old mouse.
He has a counter where you can buy a louse,
But no one comes because it's a haunted house.

He has a creaky door,
Sometimes he goes for a walk down the moor.
Although he is very poor,
He can still afford a haunted tour.

All he eats is rats and bats,
He is sometimes partial to a few cats.
He even eats a few old mats,
He sometimes eats too many fats.

But this old man is hated by all,
He'll soon get a hefty fall.
He is still very tall,
But beware, try never to meet the man that lives in the wall.

Adam Brown (13)
Carmel Technology College

A SHORT AUTUMN POEM

The hustling, bustling, rustling of the leaves
The swaying, waving, whispering of the trees
All the things that you hear here
Tell you that winter is near.

Birds prepare to fly off into the sun
And won't return till winter's on the run
Squirrels are working, their stores are low
They must collect nuts before there is snow.

Matthew Thompson (11)
Carmel Technology College

THE CURSE OF THE STONE NECKLACE

It turned day into night
And the trees looked over
Because tonight was the night of the curse
There was no sign to stay away
You just knew it anyway
When people went in
They never came out
Was it shock?
Was it horror?
That's what we're about to find out
It started as a stormy day
And turned into a stormy night
When a girl went trick or treating
And came to this house which
She knew wasn't right
They invited her in
And turned her to stone
And now she's on a necklace
Looking small and old
That's the story of the curse
Beware, you've been told.

Natalie Crowley (13)
Carmel Technology College

GETTING UP

Snug and warm, fast asleep,
Then my alarm goes bleep, bleep, bleep.
Struggle out of my cosy bed,
Bewildered thoughts still in my head.

Mam shouts 'David, are you up?'
'Yes' I reply and then I jump
Back into bed and wriggle down
Pulling my quilt all around.

No time to drift off again,
Mam's upstairs being a pain.
Reluctantly I leave my bed
With thoughts of sleep still in my head.

David Suleiman (12)
Carmel Technology College

AUTUMN

The leaves are running in a whirl
then the wind stopped blowing.
They drop to the floor
crunch, crackle they go.

Jack Frost most nights goes out
in the freezing cold weather
and glistens the streets of Darlington
with his big, long cloak.

The sun tries to peep through the heavy cloud
warming the cold, planet Earth below.

Charlotte Robinson (11)
Carmel Technology College

Autumn

Autumn is the season where woolly jumpers are worn
and the mornings are cold and foggy.

I watch the little squirrels gathering their nuts and berries,
then placing them neatly underground.

Staring out of the window I see leaves falling
and the wind carrying them far.

Jack Frost, lurking round a corner at the ready
to give you an evil taste of autumn.

The meadows are golden and rich with crops
that are gathered for a village feast.

Thinking of autumn makes me shiver inside
as a cold breeze enters my room.

Lisa Chou (11)
Carmel Technology College

Winter

I'm asleep in my room where I'm warm and safe.
When I'm woken by a blood-curdling chill.
And I see the snowflakes on the window sill.
A gush of icy wind comes rushing in an open door.
A blanket of snow covers the ground.
It sleeps there without a sound.
The flowers have died, the animals have gone.
And then I know that winter has come.

Sarah Anne Fawcett (13)
Carmel Technology College

AUTUMN

No more summer sun smiling down at me,
Jack Frost is here now bringing autumn with him.
The leaves start falling from the trees
like paratroopers going into battle.
The yellow, brown and golden leaves,
and not forgetting the red leaves,
start running around and stumbling like children playing
when you open your door.
A forlorn one may just come tumbling in . . .
and lie there exhausted on the floor.
The night before Jack Frost appeared
laying a glistening silver carpet of frost.
The spider webs are covered in the morning dew.
The shiny conkers start falling from the trees
in their prickly cases ready for a fight.
Whack, smack, *oh no crack!*
Out in the forest nuts lay clustered on the floor.
The animals and farmers battle it out
to see who can collect their harvest fastest.

Richard Blaylock (11)
Carmel Technology College

AUTUMN

The leaves are falling,
Crunching under our feet.
When you hear a thud, the conkers are falling.
The floor is crispy with the frost.
The days are getting colder.
The birds are flying away.
The plants are all dressed in rags
And Jack Frost is nipping our toes and our fingers.

Thomas Anderson (11)
Carmel Technology College

A Summer Morning In Norfolk

The sun was beaming down
The swallows were chattering on the telephone wires
The grass glinted and sparkled with dew
Tiny shiny cobwebs littered the dewy fields looking like miniature
Picnic mats spread out over the soaking grass
The trees gently danced in the breeze
A beautiful summer morning
Horses gracefully chased each other
The newly grown mushrooms were as white as cotton wool
With frilly petticoats just waiting to be picked
Chickens scratched quietly around their pen, clucking every so often
Doves cooed to each other as they flew overhead
Baby rabbits nibbled the dewy grass with their watchful parents
A beautiful, peaceful summer morning.

Emma Hall (14)
Carmel Technology College

Autumn Leaves

The leaves from the trees are golden and brown
Swaying gently down to the ground
The colours are all different, like money but cold and wet
Tomorrow is a newborn day, new leaves, new colours, foggy and grey
They crunch
They crackle
They make a loud noise
We will burn them tonight
And when the wind comes the ashes will blow
To be scattered around the land.

Helen Porter (11)
Carmel Technology College

COLD AUTUMN

Everyone's wrapped up nice and warm,
The leaves crinkle when you stand on them,
Children want to do it again and again.

All the leaves are rotting on the ground,
Hear that? There is no sound.
All the trees are bare,
About there are people everywhere.

Some leaves are clinging on the branch,
The wind is blowing harder and harder
And the leaves let go their hold.
They flutter down to the ground in flocks,
Then they lay on the floor.
When you open your door,
A tired leaf might scuttle in.

Frost is on the window sill,
Frost is on the door,
Frost is on the doorstep,
It's summer no more.

Vicky Dalton (12)
Carmel Technology College

AUTUMN

Wind is rushing and whistling through the trees,
Leaves are shivering and shaking in the breeze.
As the wind gets stronger they tumble down,
Spiralling, swirling, turning round and round.

Golden yellow, orange, brown,
A rainbow of colours dance up and down.
Children merrily run down the street,
The leaves crunch and crackle under their feet.

A Summer Morning In Norfolk

The sun was beaming down
The swallows were chattering on the telephone wires
The grass glinted and sparkled with dew
Tiny shiny cobwebs littered the dewy fields looking like miniature
Picnic mats spread out over the soaking grass
The trees gently danced in the breeze
A beautiful summer morning
Horses gracefully chased each other
The newly grown mushrooms were as white as cotton wool
With frilly petticoats just waiting to be picked
Chickens scratched quietly around their pen, clucking every so often
Doves cooed to each other as they flew overhead
Baby rabbits nibbled the dewy grass with their watchful parents
A beautiful, peaceful summer morning.

Emma Hall (14)
Carmel Technology College

Autumn Leaves

The leaves from the trees are golden and brown
Swaying gently down to the ground
The colours are all different, like money but cold and wet
Tomorrow is a newborn day, new leaves, new colours, foggy and grey
They crunch
They crackle
They make a loud noise
We will burn them tonight
And when the wind comes the ashes will blow
To be scattered around the land.

Helen Porter (11)
Carmel Technology College

COLD AUTUMN

Everyone's wrapped up nice and warm,
The leaves crinkle when you stand on them,
Children want to do it again and again.

All the leaves are rotting on the ground,
Hear that? There is no sound.
All the trees are bare,
About there are people everywhere.

Some leaves are clinging on the branch,
The wind is blowing harder and harder
And the leaves let go their hold.
They flutter down to the ground in flocks,
Then they lay on the floor.
When you open your door,
A tired leaf might scuttle in.

Frost is on the window sill,
Frost is on the door,
Frost is on the doorstep,
It's summer no more.

Vicky Dalton (12)
Carmel Technology College

AUTUMN

Wind is rushing and whistling through the trees,
Leaves are shivering and shaking in the breeze.
As the wind gets stronger they tumble down,
Spiralling, swirling, turning round and round.

Golden yellow, orange, brown,
A rainbow of colours dance up and down.
Children merrily run down the street,
The leaves crunch and crackle under their feet.

Golden fields of corn, see them gently sway,
It's harvest time - let's gather up the hay.
Migrating swallows are ready to go,
Warned by their instinct of the winter's snow.

Cathy Harris (11)
Carmel Technology College

AUTUMN IS?

Autumn is gloomy,
autumn is dull,
what's the point of autumn?
I don't know,
I don't care.
Autumn is the time of leaves falling
and birds singing no more.
I walk outside in the damp stormy weather
and I notice there's something wrong.
It's not summer anymore.
Autumn is a time for fires burning crackling.
Autumn is a time for fog that lingers in the air
and clings to the ground.
The footballers of Darlington
dance in the autumn mist.
The leaves are gathering
into armies ready to attack,
swirling, curling down to the ground.
It's time to bring out the hot chocolate again.
I'm ready for a hot bath, blissfully relaxing.
It's time for the sun to set in the sky,
lower and lower in my eye.

Stuart Cameron (11)
Carmel Technology College

My Brother, The Idiot

My brother is a total idiot,
He thinks he's the best thing since sliced bread.
He likes to think he's super cool,
When in fact he's just super sad.

My brother is a total idiot,
He actually thinks he can sing
When in actual fact he sounds like a cat
Being strangled deep underwater!

My brother is a total idiot,
He thinks he is a 'God send',
But if I were God, I'd take him back
And toss him in the pile for rejects!

My brother is a total idiot,
He thinks he's really good at football,
But the only time he ever seems to score goals
Is when he's in goal and it's for the opposition.

My brother, the idiot!

Kayley Hunter (14)
Carmel Technology College

Autumn

The crispy, crunchy golden leaves fall helter-skelter from the trees
As the leaves fall to their knees
And there goes the bees

Prepare yourself for the cold
The leaves are wet and old
And now they are starting to fold

Watch the sycamore seed and the golden leaves
Now the leaves feel the breeze
And fall crash bang to their knees

Summer is over and autumn's back
And be prepared for cold autumn's whack.

Rebecca Clarke (11)
Carmel Technology College

LIKE IT WAS JUST YESTERDAY

It had been building up for a while,
The fights, arguments, the upset.
The chats about it not being anyone's fault,
They would both still love me.
Of course I knew it would happen soon,
But when it did, it hurt,
Like a bomb had been dropped right on me,
Or a stab in the heart.
All the questions in my head still asked,
Why me? Why them? Why now?
It felt so strange, them both not there,
Only dad, mum being like a visitor.
But like they said, they both still love us,
I always knew they would.
It takes a while but eventually it gets better,
Only the odd argument or nasty words.
But even now, nearly a year gone by,
I still remember every detail,
What was said, everyone's faces, how I acted,
Like it was just yesterday.

Sophie Heywood (14)
Carmel Technology College

ENGLISH POEM

I awakened on that fateful morning,
Wishing that hell was called off today,
Satan's afternoon would soon be upon us,
Perpetual pain eating away my brain.

I entered the bus,
A roller-coaster ride down to the bottomless pit of boringness,
Jerking, bouncing, screeching round each and every corner,
Until the gates of no return sucked you into their evil wrath.

Two of their henchmen
Forcing the devil's garment onto your back,
In the overwhelming heat, as other poor lost souls enter the other realm,
Where upon prisoners were forced to jump onto people
As hard as they could just to be the holder of an egged ball.

Feeding time awaits
And as the slop awaits you,
Your curdling, rattling stomach prepares for a beating.
Many have tried to escape,
Only a handful have been successful in their task.

And so the afternoon has come, the worst possible scenario,
Double double science, the depression tablet's the only thing
That keeps us going.
Many slumber around looking for the easy way out,
As we prepare our unstable conscience for the worst word known
To the human race today; dictation, arrrrggghh!

Daniel Hanratty (14)
Carmel Technology College

THE BALLAD OF DOCTOR DEATH!

Down Manchester way,
There lived a doctor,
A friend to one and all,
Until one fine day,
When he was taken away
For murder most foul he must pay.

There was an old lady,
Down Manchester way,
Who recently passed away,
When the will was read,
Appalled at what it said,
Her daughter to the police did go.

The will it did say,
'To my doctor I'll pay,
All the money I own.'
The experts then said,
When the women was dead
The doctor did her away.

The poor woman who died,
She wasn't alone,
For graves now were opened
All over the place,
And our fine doctor friend,
His life he will spend,
Behind bars down Manchester way.

Joel Alderson (14)
Carmel Technology College

SUMMER IN FRANCE

The plane skimmed over the tarmac like a graceful swan,
Before slowing to a stop, when we exited the plane,
The heat hit us straight away and took me by surprise,
It was only France after all, but it was nearly thirty-five.

The bus took us to our site, La Baume by name,
There were palm trees and bright white walls glistening in the sun,
We found our tent and unpacked our things,
The bus hissed with a sigh of relief as the last bags were removed.

On the first day at the beach, we all looked like milk bottles,
The people all around us were brown like chocolate muffins,
The sea rolled gently over the rocks,
And the white tips sprayed over us, like twinkling glitter falling onto
                                                                                                             a picture.

We walked along the soft, hot sand in Cannes, St Tropez and Frejús,
With the sun shining brightly down on us,
We gradually went from white, to beige, to brown,
And only occasionally being burnt, but not too badly!

By the end of the fortnight we were brown and relaxed,
Ready to get back to work, life and cold, wet England,
We boarded the plane and looked back at the country below us,
Said goodbye to the lush green fields, white sandy beaches and clear
                                                                                                              blue sea.

Laura Fawcett (15)
Carmel Technology College

TILLY

Tilly is my cat,
She's soft, cute and fluffy.
Sitting all day is what she likes
And it's very rare that she fights.
Sometimes she wanders out the door,
But she doesn't wander very far.
When the mog wants to come in,
She'll sit on the top of the car and make a din.
My mother loves Tilly to bits,
But sometimes she gets on my wick.
Whine, whine, whine is what she does best,
I really do wish she'd give it a rest.
The only thing Tilly wants is attention.
If she went to school she'd always be on detention!
But however annoying the cat may be,
She's still soft, cute and fluffy.

Francesca Denham (14)
Carmel Technology College

AUTUMN

Colours, colours everywhere,
Leaves are falling in your hair.
Trees here, trees there,
Some are colourful, some are bare.
Waking up to nippy weather,
Spiders' webs glistening in the morning dew.
Golden leaves running and running, wild and free,
Autumn is the time for me.

Catherine Benson (11)
Carmel Technology College

MY MAM

My mam's called Julie
she's 39
I'll tell you about her
in 18 lines.

Curly blonde hair
big eyes of brown
always a smile
never a frown

Soft and gentle
as can be
she is always
there for me

So kind-hearted
lovely and sweet
buys me chocolates
as a treat

I love my mam
she plays a big part
I love her so
with all my heart.

Amy Flanagan (13)
Carmel Technology College

MY BEST MATE

She is tall and fair,
Has strawberry-blonde hair,
Her eyes are as blue as the sea.

Her lips are like cherries,
Her skin soft as berries,
And her nose is as perfect as can be.

Her teeth are straight,
She's so fun, it's great,
Yeah, she's my best mate.

Rebecca White (12)
Carmel Technology College

I HATE TRAVELLING!

My mum said we were going to Alton Towers,
Travelling time is about four hours.
'It would be fun,' my mum said,
But that is what all kids dread.
In the car there was my mum, my sister, me and my brother,
There again, I wouldn't swap them for any other!
After sitting sweating for hours in the car,
My mum finally said 'Here we are.'
We all jumped out ready to go,
But there's still my mum going very slow.
First ride was the Thunder Loop,
But my mum said we would bring up that soup.
We ran around like lunatics all day,
That was needless to say!
The wind was blowing in our faces,
All of us were having races!
It finally came to the end of the day,
Which I was glad to say.
Driving home was a nightmare,
No one in the car seemed to care!
We finally pulled up in our driveway,
All I heard was my mum say:

'Everyone out, we are finally home!'

Carrianne Green (14)
Carmel Technology College

WINTER

Winter had finally come.
The brown, rusty leaves of autumn were now frozen
in the sparkling snow.
The trees were bare with a small layer of snow
on the left side of each branch.
Small birds flutter around searching for stranded worms
in the snow and they are cheeping quietly.
Layers of tiny snowflakes fall down from the overcast sky like glitter,
twisting and turning like a minute ballerina to the ground.
Children played happily in the snow dressed in big warm coats
and scarves, and weaving pom-pom hats as they covered themselves
with flying snowballs.
Winter had finally come.

Duncan Harrison (14)
Carmel Technology College

PINK

Pink is gushing with a flush of warm, rich, hot colour.
Emotions loud and confident, fluttering in its own atmosphere.
It is the height of fashion, a real scorcher,
reflecting the tones of skin colour, glowing with its own power.
Touchable floridness igniting many hearts,
passion rushing to their hot heads.
Its enthusiastic emotions, a reminder of a calorific summer,
on a tropical island.
Pink is not reliable or honest, it's not pure or saintly.
It is the colour of flirtation and happy moods.
Fun's theme tune if you like.

Lucy Cooper (14)
Carmel Technology College

THE DREAM

To dream, is this time to wait.
For my forthcoming, precious chance to soar;
into the ever-changing landscape, that is the sky.
Before this century, my only chance would be to become a bird.
Until the time of Orville Wright.
He pioneered my dream.

Now I'm at the controls,
my dream is very real, waiting with baited breath,
for the pilot with his pre-flight checks;
Magnetos, oil pressure, engine temperature,
the unseen voice crackles, 'Clear for take-off.'
My dream begins once again.

I pull back on the throttle,
we reach sixty knots.
Ease back on the stick, we soar into the white heavens.
We climb, cutting through the soft border,
between the ground and the blue yonder.
My dream reaches its climax.

We loop, roll and stall,
the engine snarling at the clouds,
the great panorama below.
A clutter of ant-sized objects.
The dream must now end.

We head toward the huge scar across the landscape.
A huge blemish within the idyllic countryside.
This symbolises the end.
Lower, lower, gravity reclaims our chariot of the sky.
I wake up, I have to dream once again.

Philip Buxton (14)
Carmel Technology College

CHRISTMAS

The boxes were out, the tree was stood.
We started to open one box at a time.
First box was lights, next tinsel and baubles.
Soon every decoration was spread on the floor
waiting to be put on the tree.

First was the tinsel, then baubles, it all suddenly came to life.
The last thing we put on the tree was the lights
They ran like ivy up a wall
Then bang we hit the switch, the tree came to life at last.

The house was almost done by now,
So we started to put the presents under the tree.
By now everything was in its place,
It all looked real.

I was anxious to open presents.
As soon as I was awake I flew to open them.
Everyone was opening presents all at once
It all looked like a sea of wrapping paper.

I couldn't wait for the rest of the family to come,
I wanted to start opening presents again.
They arrived at last with arm loads of presents.
Everyone started opening again until another sea had formed.

Just as quickly as it had all started
It ended, we were packing up the decorations
And putting things away for another year.

Ruth Maddison (14)
Carmel Technology College

IN THE LIBRARY

In the library,
Standing on the spiral staircase,
Gripping the banister,
Spooky atmosphere,
Shaking with horror,
Behind the green curtain,
A ghost was hiding,
Breathing quickly,
A short interval,
He pushed me,
To the edge of the stairs,
I find a concealed doorway,
I escape.

Rachael Taylor (13)
Carmel Technology College

IVY, THE WORLD'S GREATEST NANA

Yes, it's really true, she was the greatest too!
The best you'd find, with a heart so kind
And a love that's made of gold
And as I've been told, that love's pure gold.

And yes it seems it's true,
She loved me 'til the end
And even though at the end she didn't know me,
She loved me just the same.
All the times that I was wrong, she never held it against me.
And yes I guess it's true, she was the greatest too!

Samantha Winchester (13)
Carmel Technology College

My Dad

The loud deep voice
The funny faces
They always make me laugh
His bright ginger hair
His thousands of freckles
He's like a dot to dot
I always wonder what picture he'll make
If I join them all up
He is average height
He is medium build
Just a normal man
He has bright aqua-blue eyes
They glisten in the light
He reminds me of the calm sea
He never shouts
Well not normally anyway
He has a deep laugh
A bit like a chuckle
He reminds me of Fred Flintstone
He is of course my *dad!*

Stacey Young (13)
Carmel Technology College

My Sea Poem

The turquoise waves are calm,
like a cradle rocking gently to and fro.
The waves carry things and drop
them on the shore.

The foamy waves lash,
anger spreading through them.
Howling, trying to drag you in,
off to the unknown.

The warm waters are calm,
hardly any ripple can be seen.
Children play in the sand,
while others just lie.

The stormy waves carry
the boats out to sea.
Whoosh, whoosh, the storm is dying down
until . . . everything's calm.

Sophie-Jo Quick (11)
Carmel Technology College

SHARK ATTACK

I come in the morning
I come in the night
I prey on fish that make a tasty meal
Look at me glide
Look at me swim
You try to catch me
Or I try to catch you
Look at my grey, slimy, slippery skin
See my teeth like blades of steel
Don't catch me I say
Put those nets away
Or I might try to catch you too
I hunt with style
I smell the blood from wounded fish
I hang out in the harbour where
There is plenty of grub.

Thomas Pattison (11)
Carmel Technology College

The Big Blue Wet Thing

The sea to me is like a ferocious beast
Its waves lapping over the golden, shimmering sands
But often the splashing surf tickles the children's tiny toes
The deepest emerald waters waver endlessly below

Brightly coloured beach balls bouncing and soaring
Through the sun's mustard rays
How I love the long lasting, luscious, sunny summer days

As the fluffy cotton wool gracefully glides
Over the giant egg yolk
The light blue sheet slowly
Almost unnoticeably
Darkens

The brightly coloured land boats drive away
The beach is deserted
Day 300,000,000 has come to an end
The beast lies tranquil waiting
To pounce on another day.

Laura McEvoy (12)
Carmel Technology College

Autumn

The magic of autumn is here again,
Its glory falling in red, yellow and browns.
There's a flurry of leaves like a winter's gale
And as the sun fails to come, all will be foggy and cold.
As the hedgehog scurries into the leaves,
Its instincts tell him to get away from the cold autumn breeze.
But from all of this we grin,
Awaiting winter, summer and spring.

Philip Jones (12)
Carmel Technology College

MY LIFE AT SEA

I am a mighty fish
For I am the jellyfish
I do not bite, I sting
I'll give you pain from within
I don't like being poked
I don't like being choked
Don't stand on me for
I sting worse than any bee
I am not like you, I don't have legs
And waves I can't walk through
And everywhere I go I see people petrified
But what am I to do?
I don't have flippers, wings or fins
But I can swim
I don't have arms or legs but I can move
You may be scared of me
But remember you don't have to hide
Sometimes people see me
Some people say the blue jellyfish is worse
Do believe or don't
Remember I am watching
Remember I am here
Remember I am hiding
Don't come too close or
I'll give you pain - severe!

Kashya Caplice (11)
Carmel Technology College

HELP!

I'm a small fish,
I'm all red,
I really need to hide,
Because hooks flowing on the bed.
Hurry up we must go, come on,
I'm all wanted you know!
Darting fast, follow me,
So please I ask, can you help me?

There's a shadow in the sky
And a really long stick,
A thin piece of rope
And something very thick,
I want to swim away,
I want to be free,
I've already asked but can you help me?

Look, the sun is coming out,
I love it now the shadows gone,
I'm so excited, I must shout!
Now all swimming animals galore,
Here is a party for you all to explore!
I know all my fears are not at an end,
But I must be at a party I said I would attend!

Kayley Smith (11)
Carmel Technology College

MY GRANDMA

My grandma is now shorter than me,
But when I was smaller,
She sat me on her knee.
On a Sunday, she comes round for tea,
And she really enjoys talking to me.

When she is here, bless the old dear,
She falls asleep in the chair,
She lies there snoring, what is she dreaming?
And messes up her freshly permed hair!

Katrina Busby (12)
Carmel Technology College

THE GARGOYLE

On a tangled lawn
The moon shone down
Through swaying trees and leaves.
The shadows moved in an evil dance
To make a faint heart leap.
The heavy, rusty, iron gate
Opened with a creak,
The gravel on the overgrown path
Crunched beneath my feet.
Through a covering curtain of ivy and thorn,
I fought my way through to the door,
Never opened in years, it was covered in moss,
Yet still seemed forbidding and strong.
The stone of the wall rose into the dark,
I stepped back to look out the top,
When a blinding flash lit up the night
And a terrible face looked back.
I turned on my heels,
My heart in my mouth,
My body pulsing with fear.
I never returned to the old, ruined house,
The gargoyle had driven me clear.

Josie Grierson (13)
Carmel Technology College

A Crab's Life

I am the rich and famous Sebastian the crab,
My appearance and looks have never been called drab.
I live between the rocks and in the deep, dark ocean,
My inaccurate sideways walk is my mode of motion.
I devour small creatures from the sand,
They taste quite salty but never bland.
They're not the tastiest I've eaten,
But small creatures can definitely be beaten.
I sleep hidden away in a deep rock pool,
The water is so fresh and cool.
With my anemone who sleeps by my side,
The water's rough and raging as I'm washed away by the tide.

Hannah Ramsey (11)
Carmel Technology College

The Crab

In the big blue sea,
I start looking for tea,
In a rock pool or lagoon,
It better be soon,
I will settle for shrimp,
If they are juicy and pink,
If I don't miss many,
I will probably sink,
You will see me in bed,
At the bottom of the sea,
Looking for plankton to finish my tea.

Liam Russell (11)
Carmel Technology College

THE SEA

The sand was soft and hot
it looked like bright yellow gold
As I sat down I felt it go
in-between my toes
It made my toes tingle like a feather
brushing between my little toes
I take a walk down to the sea
with the seagulls flying over me
I feel the water on my feet
so refreshing, such a treat
The day starts to come to an end
the waves don't seem to be my friend
They start to crash against the rocks
with such a force I get a shock
The sun has gone from the sky
so it's time to say goodbye.

Gemma Walker (11)
Carmel Technology College

SEA POETRY

Tiptoeing my way into the sea,
The sand is soft and is sinking me.
The hot sun is beaming down
And the rough waves crashing around.
All I can hear is squawking seagulls
And all I can smell is fish and salt.
The hot sun so bright and yellow,
It makes everyone feel very mellow.

Claire Ward (11)
Carmel Technology College

THE POEM OF MR CRAB

My pincers are large and hard
And my name is Mr Crab.
I like to eat fish sometimes seaweed,
Depends on the dish.
I like to watch children
That are splashing and splishing.
I don't like to swim, just walk sideways
Not frontwards or backwards.
I see the sun glistening in the sky
And the children packing their bats and balls away.
Now my big red coat is getting heavy
So bye for now.

Jamie Wicks (11)
Carmel Technology College

MY MUM

My mum takes care of me
And loves me
She kisses me and hugs me
Looks after me through the day
Loving me in every single way
She guides me through wrong and right
Tucks me in at night
Doesn't matter if we fight
I know she loves me deep inside
I don't know what I'd do without my mum
But there's always my dad!

Rachel Louise Murdoch (11)
Carmel Technology College

THE MIGHTY CRAB

I am Theordore the mighty crab
skittering sideways under a slab
searching the sand with my claws
hoping for something to put in my jaws.
Each wave crashes on the sea floor
with slimy seaweed and shiny shells
Oh, what's this? An old ship's bell.

Thomas Reeves (11)
Carmel Technology College

THE SHARK

Blue and grey is my colour
Large is my shape
Staring is my gaze
And razor sharp are my teeth
Swiftly swimming through the undercurrent
Without a wave or a whale to be seen
I'm full of purpose as I pursue my prey.

Beth Blake (11)
Carmel Technology College

NIGHT

N ight is darker, darker than the sky.
I love to see the moon shine.
G oing to a party all night long.
H aving midnight snacks is a midnight feast.
T he fool of darkness is coming tonight.

Louise Barras (11)
Carmel Technology College

NEVER LAND

There is a little corner
In your brain that you can't reach
It's your never-never-never land
We all have one each.

It is your little place
Where you are king or queen
Your own land of tales and stories
Where you have never been.

You can live in a castle
Or a grass hut on the shore
It is your special place
Where you will never bore.

Daniel Hall (12)
Carmel Technology College

AUTUMN

Autumn winds blowing the trees,
with a slight chilly breeze.
Cold nights, cold days,
winter's not far away.
Getting so cold you're turning blue,
if you're not careful you'll catch the flu.
Dark nights in to stay,
can't stay out long to run and play.
But when winter comes Christmas too,
then you won't be bored for things to do.

Adam Grieve (11)
Carmel Technology College

THE MOON

Rising gently to guard the night
Until the break of morning light
Sitting up there in the sky
Like a sentinel way on high.

When you look out from your bed
The moon's still up there overhead
And when the world is all at peace
The moon is shining, never to cease.

Bright and clear to show the way
Until the golden glow of day
And when I rise at the crack of dawn
The moon has vanished from the morn.

Thomas Eldrington (11)
Carmel Technology College

MY BEDROOM

One day we were visited by my Aunty Bessy
Who said my bedroom was far too messy.
My bedroom is tiny and far too small
For a girl who is growing big and tall.
Outside my window is a countryside view
With lots of cows that all go *moo*.
I have a wooden bed
With a rounded head,
Or at least so my mother said.
Overall, my bedroom is so full of junk,
Everyone is surprised I have not yet sunk.

Jenny Bell (11)
Carmel Technology College

Autumn

In autumn the leaves fall
from the trees,
And we start to feel a
chilly breeze.

The days seem shorter as
we're blocked out from light,
By the creepy dark
and dismal night.

The animals curl up tight
and sleep,
Through autumn and winter
without a peep.

Claire Richardson (11)
Carmel Technology College

Autumn Time

All the leaves are turning brown,
The summer's gone, it's time to frown.
The clouds are low and dull and grey,
As autumn brings a shorter day.
The leaves are yellow, red and brown,
Soon they will be floating down.
The weather is cold, windy and wet,
The snow is not upon us yet.
We made the most of the springtime's fun,
We made the most of the summer's sun,
We still have memories of holidays away,
When everything was bright, happy and gay.

Catherine McKeown (12)
Carmel Technology College

Doughnuts

If your tummy starts to rumble,
Don't think of pizza or apple crumble,
Pop to the baker (you know what I mean?)
And buy a doughnut - that's my dream!
There are many different types of them,
Sizes large and small.
They're fat, they're round, get five for a pound,
Then stand and scoff them all.
Some have sprinkles on the top, others dipped in cinnamon,
The sugary ones are awfully nice
And I love the ones with jam in 'em.
You can have them after breakfast or while you watch the news
And if you squeeze them rather soft you'll see the goodness ooze.
But when you pop off down to Gregg's and wipe out every shelf,
Be sure no matter what you do to think about yourself.
I know that you don't like the sound of salad on a plate,
But when you're sad about your size it's really far too late!

Christopher McGovern (12)
Carmel Technology College

The White Whale

I am Bob the whale and I am about 23m long.
I am fast, big and strong so just leave me alone and let me eat in peace.
I wish I could live without being harpooned at.
Remember, I am longer than you and I can destroy you
and your ship so just leave me alone or I will come for you.
I am faster than a shark and I can come racing for you
and with the wink of an eye you will be dead.
So just leave me in peace, to eat alone and live.

Stuart Brennan (11)
Carmel Technology College

THE WOODS

Darkness descends lightly on the trees,
the ghostly white moon rises high into the sky.
Stars twinkle against the pitch-black blanket,
the last light in a nearby town goes off
and everything is silent except
for the sound of the rushing river nearby.
An owl takes off into the night and hovers high
above the trees searching for its prey.
A mouse scuttles and scampers about keeping under the shadows
trying to remain out of predators' eyes.
Hours go by, the moon gently goes down,
the stars fade to nothing and vanish,
the sun comes up to conquer the night.
A car passes by,
terrified birds take to flight.
A rooster crows in the distance,
as the milkman makes his daily rounds.
Morning descends over the town and countryside
as night retreats to its shadowy hiding place.

Michelle Tsang (13)
Carmel Technology College

AUTUMN

The reds and browns go whirling down
The oranges and golds sail through the sky
As though they have no weight
They twist and twirl, dazzle and whirl all the way down
The ground is now a sheet of leaves, a blanket of pretty colours
Autumn is a colourful time but also kind of cold and nippy.

Andrew McElvaney (11)
Carmel Technology College

TRAINERS

I love trainers a whole lot,
they keep my feet cool
when days are hot.
All my six pairs
are under lock.
You see loads of nice shoes,
but who cares?
'Cos trainers rock,
trainers really do rock,
which ones do I wear?
Nike, Adidas, Fila or Reebok?

Trainers are cool,
when you wear them
you look trippy.
It's a bad idea to wear them
in a swimming pool.
You can even wear trainers
if you're a hippy!
'Cos trainers rule the world!

Nadia Piper (13)
Carmel Technology College

WHEN YOU DON'T KNOW HOW YOU FEEL

When you don't know how you feel,
walk on grass and you will feel
silence and peace at last.
Stars shine brightly through the night,
sun shines brightly through the day,
now I feel OK.

Charlotte Oldham (12)
Carmel Technology College

Chocolate

Chocolate comes in various colours
And in various flavours as well.
It's white and milky and dark and brown,
And orange, all aromas to smell.

Chocolate is sweet and dreamy
And it's all shapes and sizes too.
It's either a yard of Cadbury's
Or a Santa, a teddy, a shoe!

Chocolate is perfectly scrumptious,
It's got all different labels you see,
Bourneville, Cadbury and Nestlé,
But it's got to be Terrys for me.

Chocolate is gorgeously creamy,
The texture just melts down your throat.
The problem is chocolate's quite fattening,
Stop eating or you'll not fasten your coat.

Danielle Hossell (12)
Carmel Technology College

Autumn

Autumn, autumn has come,
Parents running round for fun,
For conkers have fallen and
Squirrels are hunting.

Autumn, autumn has come
It's like children with new toys,
And summer is no more.

William Barras (12)
Carmel Technology College

AUTUMN DAYS

On a cold, misty day,
Golden leaves drifted where they lay.
Dry and papery they swirl,
Until they drop discarded to the ground.

Green hues changed
To red and bronze,
Like an army
Of skeletons on the ground.

Crunching and scrunching
Under your feet, wind-blown sails
Collect under your seat.

Bare and stark
The tree looks down
At all its scattered children
On the ground.

Sarah Hullah (12)
Carmel Technology College

DEEP DANGER

The water is cool,
The water is deep,
Beneath the waves the fishes eat.
The seaweed sways from side to side
And through its branches the fishes glide.
Danger lurking in the rocks,
Hungry sharks are ready to shock.
Little fishes best beware,
For hungry sharks are everywhere.

Sophie Knapton (11)
Carmel Technology College

AUTUMN

Autumn is the time between summer and winter,
the change from one extreme to another.
Autumn is the time when golden leaves blow,
falling to the ground which they then smother.
Autumn is the time up to Hallowe'en,
cold, wet weather in-between.
But when it comes,
All Hallows Eve,
it's scarier than you could believe.
But would we have this without autumn?
Who could imagine Hallowe'en
in another season?

Jenny Redmond (12)
Carmel Technology College

AUTUMN 1999

Animals foraging for winter food,
Humans getting into the autumn mood.
We all gradually get shaky knees,
As the leaves fall gracefully from the trees.
We wake up to find wet ground,
We are not surprised at the moisture we've found.
We all put on our woolly hats,
Step out of the door and wish we had fur, like cats.
We all hope for an award of platinum,
For getting ready for the new millennium.

Elinor Campbell (13)
Carmel Technology College

AUTUMN

Leaves begin to fall from trees,
Slowly drifting down.
Brown, orange, auburn,
That's the colour they change.
Crunch, crush, crunch.

The weather gets cooler,
The nights get darker,
Wind blows swiftly,
Doors bang loudly.

Hallowe'en's coming,
Bonfire night too.
Fireworks, bangers, bonfires,
Witches and goblins too.

It's not time for snowmen,
Sledges, scarves or hats,
But as the summer sun goes down,
The autumn moon comes up.

Lisa McCallion (12)
Carmel Technology College

AUTUMN

It's autumn.
The sun is down, the leaves are brown and falling.
The cold and snow are coming with winter.

Birds chirp, squirrels scurry, running around in a hurry
To find acorns, for the winter is coming.

Stuart Luff (12)
Carmel Technology College

BLUE

Blue is the sky when it's a lovely sunny day.
Blue are the icicles on a frozen pond in the cold winter.
Blue is a dolphin swimming in the lovely blue sea.
Blue is the eyeshadow on B*witched, the band.
Blue is a bluebird as it flies across the land.
Blue is this pen as it writes this poem.

Karma McElvanna (11)
Carmel Technology College

AUTUMN

A   utumn is here.
U   nder the trees, there's lots of leaves.
T   elling my friends it is oh so cold.
U   nhappy about the freezing world.
M   ore leaves are falling.
N   ow autumn is here.

Leanne Rolfe (12)
Carmel Technology College

AUTUMN

A   utumn is the time of the year I love most.
U   mbrellas come out because of the rain.
T   wigs are all that are left on the trees.
U   nder the bed of leaves, there is grass ready for the next summer.
M   ost of the leaves are getting turned from green to brown.
N   ow autumn has gone, the snow will soon be here.

Callum Rose (12)
Carmel Technology College

AUTUMN

Autumn time when the weather picks up a breeze,
Autumn time when the leaves start to fall off the trees,
Yellow, orange, brown and some are still green,
All the autumn colours can be seen.

Lots of conkers fall to the ground,
All the little boys are outward bound
To collect the conkers to play their games
And call each other silly names.

Hallowe'en is nearly here,
So let's put on our masks and spread some fear.
Witches, goblins and spirits come around,
Make sure you keep your feet firmly on the ground.

Catherine Stokell (12)
Carmel Technology College

AUTUMN POEM

The leaves are starting to fall
And conkers are for all.

Then it's here, it's Hallowe'en,
But I'm too old, I'm thirteen.

It's come to the day for the fire
And masks are out for hire.

We're all going to scare our grans,
And then we'll have loads of fans.

Well, it's time for me to go,
I hope I'll see you in the snow.

Alec Bowman (13)
Carmel Technology College

BIRTHDAYS

Birthdays come once a year,
A day to remember, the day you were born.
Wrapping paper and ribbons,
Surprises and smiles,
Presents and toys,
Best wishes and cards.

Excitement, joy, anticipation,
Full of happiness, full of fun,
Waiting for your birthday to come.

Friends come round for food and drink,
Chocolate, pizza, crisps and cake.
Glasses full of squash and Coke,
Chatting and singing . . .
'Happy birthday to you!'

Joanna Reed (13)
Carmel Technology College

WINTER

Winter is the best of all,
When the snow begins to fall.
Snowballs flying everywhere,
In your face and in your hair.
It's by far my favourite season,
Sliding around for no reason.
Then the spring just spoils it all,
Snow replaced by rainfall.

Sam Ferguson (12)
Carmel Technology College

NIGHT

It's dark outside.
It's black, pitch-black.
Scary like horror.
Like red fire in the misty air.
The cold night brings death.
As my breath leaves my mouth, the chill comes
And slowly goes down my spine.
I shiver and say,
'That's why night is night.'
Then I go inside and it hits me.
Heat, the soothing heat.
Now there's no cold.
There's just heat!

Jason McSherry (12)
Carmel Technology College

WHITE

White is the dove perched on a
branch on a cold winter's night.
White are snowflakes falling from the
misty clouds in the grey sky.
White is the empty hallway of the
spooky mansion.
White is the snowman made on
Boxing Day.
White is coldness, making your teeth
chatter
White is the ceiling you gaze upon
just before you drift off to sleep.

Sophie Boyle (11)
Carmel Technology College

WEIRD TALES

On a cliff there is a haunted house
called Wide Stone Mouse.
Doors start creaking and screams start forming.
Every time you move,
Ghosts' footsteps start to groove.
In the kitchen, there is something happening.
There seems to be someone laughing.
Large bangs of thunder and lightning,
Things move on their own
Which can also be very frightening.
In the bedroom above your head,
There seems to be blood there instead.
Wind starts howling,
Ghosts start scowling.
Don't enter unless you can take the score,
So be aware.

Joanne Charlton (13)
Carmel Technology College

HOUSE FROM HELL

Creaky doors,
Squeaky floors,
Whispering voices,
Quiet noises
Rocking chairs,
Never-ending stairs,
Scattering rats,
Dusty mats
Don't dare tell
About the house from hell.

Oliver Harker (13)
Carmel Technology College

THE PLACE WHERE THE LAUGHTER DIED

As the swing stopped,
The laughter died,
The boy laid on the floor,
Just a gust of wind. That's all it took
To kill the lanky child.

As the wind howled through the trees
And the gate screeched and squealed,
The storm was getting worse and worse
And the boy child came alive.

From the left to the right, he flew through the trees,
With a boom and a bang he landed,
Next to the swing where he'd met his fate,
Next to the place he'd died.

The swing still swings in the breeze,
The gate still screeches and squeals,
And the boy still visits the place,
The place where the laughter died.

Sarah Hancocks (13)
Carmel Technology College

AUTUMN'S HERE

Leaves falling off the trees, brown, red and green,
it's approaching Hallowe'en.
Christmas decorations appear in streets.
The scurrying of squirrels' feet,
as they wildly run around
collecting acorns from the ground.
Children going bonkers
running around collecting conkers.

Alexander Hardy (12)
Carmel Technology College

THE BANSHEE

On a cold and eerie moor
my father told to me
there's a beast out there
in the eerie air,
waiting for you and me.

No soul has ever seen it,
but out there it must be,
in the black of night
and out of sight,
waiting for you and me.

You can hear the howl in the darkness,
but the beast you will not see.
You can smell the fear,
but all you hear
is the cry of the wild banshee.

Andrew Hickson (14)
Carmel Technology College

AUTUMN

Autumn is here,
It's that time of year.
Red, brown, gold,
Brrrrr. It's getting cold.

Knocking are my knees,
Leaves are falling off the trees.
Soon it will all end,
Then snow the winter will send.

Rachel Cassidy (12)
Carmel Technology College

THE BEAST

On a stormy night,
With lightning striking everywhere.
In an old, abandoned eerie mansion
The door creaked and footsteps were heard,
But no one was there.
No rats, no mice,
But there was a legend of a beast
That ate your hands and then your feet,
So you can't move.
It would eat you
As slowly as it could,
Then it finishes you off,
Screaming in agony,
For it to stop.

Michael Rumfitt (13)
Carmel Technology College

THE MYTH OF MYSTERY

He stops and turns around at you,
He smiles that dreaded smile.
He comes forward
And spreads his arms around you
And your fears turn to tears
Of this dreaded man.
He drags and pulls you,
But then a man comes
And the abductor has gone,
Vanished into thin air.

Marc Smith (13)
Carmel Technology College

BURTY'S HOUSE

It was an old dusty house
I think there might be a mouse.

It was dark and dirty in the house,
I think the owner's name was Burty Rell.

It was a strange and eerie house,
In wonder where's that mouse?

What's that dirty smell?
It might be Burty Rell.

What's that ghoulish sound?
It's only a foolish hound.

Oh my God, it's Burty,
I hope I don't get dirty.

I think he is going to kill me,
What's this? He is billing me.

Oh my God, I have to pay rent.
I'm going to live in a tent.

Matthew Pease (13)
Carmel Technology College

SNOWFLAKES

The snowflake landed on the girl's nose,
She had to cross her eyes to see it,
It sparkled in the winter sun,
And then melted away.

The glass was frosted over,
Upon the windowpane,
It cracked and made small patterns,
Jack Frost is here again.

The time of snow's a-coming,
Snowballs and snowmen alike,
Got you, *ha*, don't try to run,
See the icicle form a spike.

Saskia van Vlijmen (12)
Carmel Technology College

THE GHOST

I live in the attic amongst the cobwebs and gloom,
Outside the bare, ancient trees in the shadows loom,
And the thunder clashes and the rain lashes down
On the old house on the hill in a desolate part of town.
It once had an owner, but I scared him away,
One hundred years ago on this very day.
As he entered my house, the door slammed behind him,
Greeted by screams, and all the lights then went dim.
The living room was like nothing he'd ever seen.
The pictures' eyes moved and their mouths were grinning mean.
Don't sit in the armchair, it'll take you below,
Down to the basement where nobody goes,
Where the ghosts rest in eternal sleep,
Their wailing a sign that away you must keep.
The kitchen is a torture chamber,
The cooking utensils took care of my neighbour.
He ran from the house into the night,
Screaming and yelling and shaking with fright.
Now I'm just waiting for another victim to come,
So I can give them the shivers and scare them numb.
But I doubt that anyone else will stop
To visit the house on the old hilltop.

Laura Wake (13)
Carmel Technology College

HOUSE OF THE DEAD

The storm came lashing down,
The lightning lighting up the night sky,
The thunder howling away,
The thought of death came trembling over me.
And there I saw it,
In the distance, the house that everybody fears,
The house of the dead,
The old, rugged house on the Hill of the Head.
I walked towards it in fear of fright,
For I thought a vampire could attack and bite,
I arrived at the door,
Panic, the door squeaked open and then slammed shut,
Help!
I walked forward and went into the dining room,
There in the corner where the piano was
I found a broom.
I turned around and looked back,
The broom was gone.
I was really scared and went out of the room.
Then I heard a clatter of pots and pans,
I walked towards the kitchen,
And there it was, the ghost's head.
I ran out of the door into the pounding storm,
never to go again to the house of the dead,
On the Hill of the Head.

David Cornforth (13)
Carmel Technology College

THE CASTLE OF MYSTERY

Creak went the door
When it opened to us all,
The night was bleak
And so was the hall.
The portraits seemed to watch you,
Those great portraits on the wall.
The castle was so huge
And you felt so small!

'It's built on a witches' burial ground,'
My father used to say,
'You mustn't ever go in there,
Neither at night, nor day.
The rain always rained there,
The lightning always struck,
Thunder can be heard,
And if you're caught . . . good luck!'

'Be caught by who?'
I used to ask,
But he would never tell me,
It seemed too much of a task!
I'd heard that he'd once been there,
Many years ago,
But what had he seen there,
Did anybody know?

Andrew McKenzie (13)
Carmel Technology College

HAUNTED HOUSES

So many stories have been told
Of houses which are always cold,
Today there is a similar thing,
Where frightening banshees are out to sing,
Shrieks of horror and shrieks of fright,
And creatures of horrific sight,
In the moon sits one of these,
Among the many howling trees,
The lightning flashes, the thunder booms,
Through and through its dingy rooms,
It is so cold, so very cold,
To enter would be oh so bold,
But if you do it is to hold
The story that is always told.

Jonathan Gunnell (13)
Carmel Technology College

WHAT'S BEHIND THE CURTAIN?

I pushed aside the curtain, and screamed,
I saw shadows of feet coming towards me,
I was scared!
I yelled for help, there was no reply,
I ran for freedom,
I got nowhere.
I was lost, lost in an old, abandoned gallery,
The wind blew,
A bat flew.
I saw a white figure in front of me,
I leaped, ran and escaped.

Vicky Warden (13)
Carmel Technology College

THE GRAVEYARD

Everything is dark, dark.
The street lights are flickering, trying to stay alive.
Trees are swaying, trying to catch me,
Hands, fingers, stretching,
Trying hard to get me
And not let me go.
The headstones glare at me, watching.
Bang!
The church doors thump together.
The wind lashing against my face,
The rain being chucked against the floor,
Then bouncing back up at me.
In the church, candles are in the window,
Gentle voices singing for me,
Why are they praying for me?
I can hear high notes,
Bats flying around, but where are they?
Something coming, coming right for me.
'Run! Run!' I hear somebody say.

Catherine Harrison (13)
Carmel Technology College

AUTUMN

Golden leaves falling off the old conker tree,
The wind howling and pounding against the houses,
And banging and hammering at the door.
Lightning crashing and bashing.
Children laughing and bashing their shiny conkers.
Animals fetching leaves, nuts and berries in time
For their long hibernation period.

Alan Barr (12)
Carmel Technology College

THE HAUNTED HAT SHOP

On a winter morning in 1896,
When the streets were paved with snow,
To 27 Chronicle Street
In time that's where we'll go.
An old man by the counter,
Manning the old shop,
Worries about his business
As no one comes to stop.
Soon the hat shop had to close,
The old man passed away,
Now the year is '99,
The shop still stands today.
The dark and gloomy hat shop,
The roof begins to fall,
No draught but it is chilling,
As shadows climb the wall.
The lonely echoing footsteps,
Cobwebs clinging to the last,
Choking in the dust bytes,
Stuck inside the past.
As you leave the hat shop,
You'll be in for quite a scare,
If you turn round and you look back,
You'll find the shop's not there.

Lizzie Jones (13)
Carmel Technology College

EXCUSES

Leanne couldn't do her homework,
She fell and hurt her hand.
Daniel didn't have time for his,
He was playing with the band.
Samantha's was eaten by her dog,
And Vicky's by her cat,
And as always from Max it's
'Did we have homework? Honest, I didn't know that!'
James was late for geography,
He was looking for his coat.
Amy's lost her workbook,
She's even got a note.
Rachel has got athlete's foot,
She cannot do PE.
Sammy says she's got it too,
How thick can teachers be?
Daniel is a mastermind at making up excuses,
Amy's forged excuse notes for twenty different uses.
Sam and Rachel's athlete's foot is all their own invention.
But still, it's those who tell the truth that land up in detention.

Ruth McGuckin (13)
Carmel Technology College

AUTUMN

Golden and crisp,
The leaves lie on the frosty,
Glistening ground,
Waiting, waiting, for final decay.
And now the whirling, misty fog
Attacks the world with its icy grip.

Becky Lane (11)
Carmel Technology College

ALONE!

A cold, silent, little boy,
quietly breathing,
as white as the snow,
newly laying on the ground.
Casting an eerie shadow
cool, gentle breeze coming through
the open window.
A coldest feeling,
his small, dark, hollow eyes
glaring, glancing all around him.
Tiny silver droplets of tears
pattering to the floor
leaving small, shimmering puddles.

Samantha Barker (13)
Carmel Technology College

THE FEATHER

Feather in the breeze
floating over trees,
swooping high and low,
viewing all below.
Speeding, slowing,
not knowing where you're going.
Diving, swirling,
swooping, curling,
is there no end to your journey,
until the breeze stops
and you rest.

Rory Grierson (11)
Carmel Technology College

Autumn

A ll around us leaves are falling,
U p above the birds are calling.
T urning brown, the leaves are dead.
U nder trees, they're brown and red.
M any of us will fear the storm.
N ow is the time to wrap up warm.

I n the cold, we'll stay inside.
S ummer dreams are far behind.

C onker fights have now begun,
O pening up the winter fun.
M oonlight shines to show us the way,
I n the streets where we still play.
N early winter, that's the way.
G rowing colder every day.

Philip McDonald (11)
Carmel Technology College

Fireworks

F is for the fireworks lighting up the beautiful blue sky,
I is for the inferno that is caused by the roaring fire,
R is for the roar that the crowds make.
E is for the electrifying feeling as you hear the fireworks bang,
W is for the work it takes to light the fireworks,
O is for the opportunity to see lots of beautiful colours
R is for the redness of the bonfire,
K is for the kids smiling with delight,
S is for the sound of the fireworks in the night.

Samuel Foster (11)
Carmel Technology College

Autumn

Autumn is brown,
Autumn is cold,
There are leaves everywhere you go.
Conker fights bring delight,
Children laugh and sing.

Look out, people run away,
Because winter is on its way!

Blissful fires bring great cheer,
On a cold autumn's night,
When Jack Frost comes and bites little bums,
And frightens children away.

A layer of ice or maybe more,
Is a sign to the birds to go.

Scuttling leaves on the floor,
Wondering where to go,
When a gust of wind comes and
Lifts them off the floor.

Autumn is bright,
As bright as candlelight
And can sometimes be dull,
Like a dark winter's night.

Now it's time to turn the lights on,
Because summer's gone.

Sophie Weddell (11)
Carmel Technology College

Autumn

Golden brown leaves on the frosty trees.
The whack of conkers hitting each other.
Animals and farmers are harvesting the crisp crops.
The race is on between the farmers and animals
To gather food for the winter.
The birds fly south to places far away and warm,
The squirrels' fur is like the dark, grey clouds,
Scudding across the autumn sky.
Jack Frost lurks around every corner
Autumn is the coming of winter.
Colours are changing like a comic strip.
Birds chirp their merry songs of peace.
The grass ices over
From the touch of Jack Frost.
Berries and logs rotting silently.
The prettiest flowers die slowly,
All because of the coming of the harsh season
Of winter.

Daniel Hustwick (11)
Carmel Technology College

The Ghost Train Gone Wrong

My friends and I went to the fair,
A ghost train was there.
I'd heard a tale about this train,
All my friends said the same.
We dared to go and have a ride,
But something spooky was inside.
As the lights went out and ghosts appeared,
All my friends had disappeared!

Rebecca Wright (13)
Carmel Technology College

AUTUMN

The leaves are swirling and twirling from the trees,
I feel a cold breeze,
He blows them,
Controls them,
The branches are whipped about,
Whispering to the trees,
He boasts his power,
The leaves are red and brown and gold,
Falling because they are now old.
Jack Frost makes the leaves crispy under my feet,
And I squash the soft berries as I walk down the street,
Children have conker fights in the dull, dark park,
It's autumn, time for the harvest.

Patrick Wake (11)
Carmel Technology College

AUTUMN

As I walk to school,
The golden brown leaves crunch under my feet.
The old, bare trees stare blankly at me.
I can see shiny, brown conkers,
That have just popped out of their prickly shells
While lying on the glistening ground.
I stand watching the little squirrels,
Collecting acorns to store away for winter days.
The swirling mist surrounds the school,
It's so thick I feel blind.
At night, Jack Frost visits our garden,
Killing all the plants,
While the birds are migrating to another land.

Lisa Hall (11)
Carmel Technology College

UNDER THE BED

Every night I go to bed,
Silly ideas get into my head.
When mum tucks me in and turns the light off,
The walls around me start to whisper, scream and cough.
I've been worrying about this moment all day,
When monsters in my room come out to play.
Behind the curtains, in the cupboard, under the bed,
It doesn't sound like they've been fed.
Grunts and groans,
Growls and moans,
Perhaps tomorrow won't be the same,
Or will it be this spooky old game?

Daniel Robson (13)
Carmel Technology College

MY DAD

I think my dad is massive,
I hold his thumb because his hand is too big.
He reads to me every night,
The books make me laugh.
I don't like going to sleep at night,
My dad sits by my bed,
I hold his thumb and he waits.
I don't know when he leaves,
He must slip away silently
When he knows I'm asleep.
He's not there in the morning.

Gillian McGuigan (13)
Carmel Technology College

TRICK OR TREAT

Creeping through the dark, grim night
Something's behind me, it's floaty and white.
Through the graveyard, I hear a distant howl,
A scream, some footsteps and a hooting owl.

Round a dark corner, up some steps,
There it stood so black, I leapt.
It's yellow eyes just glared at me
And then it fluttered to a tree.

To the creaking door I crept,
At the house where the witch she slept.
The cobwebs brushed me as I passed,
My heart was thudding, loud and fast.

I knocked at the door with a loud rat-tat,
The witch she came in her pointed hat.
My voice it trembled, 'Can I have a sweet?'
'Tonight's the night for trick or treat!'

Josie Miller (13)
Carmel Technology College

THE GRAVEYARD

The graveyard is a scary place,
It's full of emptiness and gloom,
It all seems to go to waste,
None of the trees are ever in bloom.

The graves are all going to rot,
The ivy is taking over,
It's always cold and never hot,
When you go there, you need a four-leaf clover.

At night-time, moonlight filters in,
Casting eerie shadows along the ground.
Owl's hoot making a spooky din,
And in the trees bats hang around.

Morning breaks with rolling mists,
The frost comes with a chill,
The scene takes on a different twist,
And everything is still.

Emma Rowlinson (13)
Carmel Technology College

THE GHOSTLY BOY

I find myself standing
in a dark and damp room.
There's a huddled figure,
Ghostly and small.
Spiders' webs cover me
From head to toe.
He looks up at me with his sad, red eyes,
His face is pale and thin.

He's dressed in clothes from olden days
His arms tied behind his back,
I ask 'What are you doing here?'
He gave me no reply.
His body is transparent, a faint and
Misty glow,
I hear a slam, I turn to see,
The ghost is now in front of me.

Aimee Campion (13)
Carmel Technology College

My Dog, Mindy!

Today is my birthday,
I'm six years old.
My present is Mindy,
A puppy that's mine to own.

Outside the rain is falling,
But that can't make me sad.
Soon she will be home with me,
And then I will be glad.

We got her from the breeder's home,
She's sweet and cute,
And very small.

Her sister Molly
Is my nanna's dog.
She's up and playing
As soon as she is home.

Mindy is a different matter,
She lays in bed,
Scared and timid,
Wanting to be alone.

Not long later,
She is up,
Playing with her sister
And enjoying our love.

Rachel Armstrong (13)
Carmel Technology College

THE STORM

It is an ink-black summer's night,
The stars are sparkling, glistening bright.
The moon is gleaming, full and round.
I can hear the wind calling,
Shouting out to me.
It is touching me.
I can feel a cold shiver go down my spine.
There is a man following me, but I don't want to look.
I feel a sharp pain quiver down my leg.
I stop. I cannot walk any further.
I can see a dark figure standing before me.
I feel something on my head.
I look up. It is rain.
The drops look like diamonds glistening in the darkness.
A storm is brewing up.
The wind starts to pick up more power.
I look behind me. The person has disappeared.
I ask myself, 'Where could he have gone?'
I start to run with all my strength,
Pushing against the wind.
I feel trapped. I think, 'Will I ever get out?'
There is a deep, deadly silence.
Suddenly - bang - a loud clap of thunder.
It is darting through the sky.
The houses light up with a zigzag of lightning.
I run like the wind.
'Hurry, hurry,' I shout inwardly,
Then I am home.

Rachel Baker (14)
Carmel Technology College

BEHIND THE CURTAIN

Behind the curtain,
There's a large oak case, a boy resting on it.
His skin is white as snow-covered ground,
His eyes as icy-blue as the sky in winter,
he's backing up against the wall,
Wood-panelled and hard, and snakes of red, green and orange slither.
I can see his clothes are grey and old,
Dull and dirty,
The sprinkled dust is slowly drifting in eerie light,
This ghostly looking boy moves,
I can hear his cold whispering voice,
Breaking the still silence.
I ask a question,
There's no answer.
I feel a draught as it drifts over me,
And the boy gives a faint, distant sigh.
I look up to see the salty tears pricking his sad eyes,
I feel sorry for him.
He's floating towards me now,
Then, as suddenly as a flash of lightning, he mysteriously vanishes,
Leaving me speechless . . .

Felicity Cooper (13)
Carmel Technology College

BLUE

Blue is the colour of the sky.
Blue is the colour of my best friend's eyes.
Blue is the name of my dog.
Blue is the colour of my best frock.

Leanne Knight (13)
Carmel Technology College

THE HAUNTED PAINTING

I am alone,
alone in a dark, gloomy library.
The bookcases rise above my head,
casting their shadows upon me.
There is a green, velvet curtain in front of me.
I walk towards it,
push it aside.
It is heavy and a cloud of dust rises
leaving behind a musty, stale smell.

This reveals a hard, antique oak, wooden door.
I walk towards it, push, and it gives out an enormous creak.
I poke my head around the door,
curious but careful,
eager to find out what is on the other side.

I look around,
I see . . . a bright light, flickering in the gloom,
I approach it slowly, I find,
a corridor lit with candles.
I walk quickly down the tiled, cold floor of the corridor,
my footsteps echoing in the distance.
As I do . . . I see,
broken mirrors and paintings of men in suits,
the kind with the eyes who follow and watch you
wherever you are.
I still hear whimpering, it gradually gets louder.
It is coming from the paintings.

Natalie Boyle (14)
Carmel Technology College

My Poem About Autumn

The rustling of the leaves amazed me;
The leaves falling helplessly in the wind.
It was a cool autumn Sunday and the
Sun was rising. It was a wonderful sight.
It inspired me to write this poem.
Hallowe'en is the best time in autumn for me.
Trick or treat and penny for Hallowe'en.
Conkers are the new rave,
Everyone desperately tries to win,
But I know I'm the best.
Bonfire night's in autumn.
Roasting marshmallows by the fire.
The trees are starting to get bare now,
And we're getting ready for Christmas.

Michael Brennan (13)
Carmel Technology College

Snakes Are All Slimy And Sliggery

We bought a snake for a 13th birthday,
She was all slimy and sliggery,
So we lost her in a vent,
We found her and put her back.

But she wasn't happy,
She laid some eggs, but they went yellow.
I wonder if she'll lay some more,
Let's see tomorrow.

Terrianne Hauxwell (12)
Carmel Technology College

STRANGE DESTINATIONS

Evacuees trooped to the crowded stations,
preparing to go to unknown destinations.

They have gas masks in boxes,
strung over bony shoulders,
they're starting to feel as heavy as boulders.

Hundreds of steam trains pull up to
hundreds of stations, to a sorrowful nation.

They board the train feeling stressed and in pain,
the trains pull away from crowded stations,
as the passengers wave goodbye to a tearful nation.

Their little hearts beat in time with the train's,
as the rain drips down the condensed windowpane.
To strange destinations they travel,
feeling only heartache and pain.

A thousand worlds away from their sorrowful parents,
will they ever see their children again?

They're feeling terrible, nauseous and they're in a daze,
the factories and shops and the rolling hills and forests
all go by in a haze.

Arriving in strange places, to all the foreign faces,
coming off the train, meeting new people again and again.

The parents go home to the empty houses,
there's only empty spaces where their children have been.
Will they ever see their children again?
Will they ever see them again?

Hannah Carr (12)
Carmel Technology College

THE HOO TRAIN!

Sun's rays hit the station,
it's time for evacuation.
Screams, shouts, dummies spat out - owww!
That was a loud shout.

I see a sheep eating grass
As I pass Black Valley Pass.
Oh my God, that's green,
green grass!

I arrived at my unknown destination.
I ran rapidly out of the station.
A man shouted 'Be patient.'
That's a bit much aggravation.

'Oh I see, you must be Mr Tom,
who shouted me on
when all hope was gone.
Thanks Mr Tom.'

Michael Hayman (12)
Carmel Technology College

MY DAD

When I go to bed he will come,
Come up after me,
Tuck me in,
Give me a kiss,
Sing me to sleep.
His voice is deep but not scary,
He is the greatest singer
In the world,
My dad.

Elizabeth Smyth (13)
Carmel Technology College

THE JOURNEY

At the moment, war is topic of conversation,
As I left to my unknown destination.

As I stood with my one suitcase in my hand,
There were no more seats so I had to stand.

I had to be very obedient,
As it was all a lot of excitement.

I had to be very patient,
As I jumped out of the train at the station.

I'm glad I'm escaping from the devastation,
As I thought to myself leaving the station.

Children had tears running down their faces,
They were all leading off to different places.

I felt a bit queasy about staying with a stranger,
I hoped they were kind so I wouldn't be in danger.

I was still a bit sad about leaving my home,
As I was worried about being alone.

I'd noticed everyone had friends but me,
It's not very nice to be an evacuee.

Claire Wilson (12)
Carmel Technology College

EVACUATION DAY

Here I am, going to the station,
I'm on my way to my unknown destination.
Oh look, here's the train.
I'm on my way to educate my brain.

The chimney stack goes puff, puff,
And the pistons go chuff, chuff.
The wheels go click, click on the track,
When I get there, my suitcase I'll unpack.

I've arrived here,
I'm stopping with this man, he looks a bit queer.
My first meal of the day was made by this man,
It was bacon, fried in a frying pan.

This man has ghostly white hair,
If it's anything about me, he certainly seems to care.
This man is so extremely boring,
When he goes to bed you can hear him snoring.

I've had my say,
It's been quite a day,
Now I've gone to bed
To rest my heavy head.

Anthony Savage (12)
Carmel Technology College

A STRANGE DAY

In the dark streets of London,
a small boy packs his case.
He's thin, weak and scared,
with no clue of what will soon take place.

He is on his way to the station,
he has his own label around his neck.
He has only one suitcase to last him
longer than a week.

He's waiting at the station
for the train to take him to his
unknown destination.
He hears the train coming.

He sees a big, black monster,
it has steam coming out of it,
it nearly gave him a fit.

It's suddenly all gone quiet,
no shouts or squalls can be heard,
apart from the mothers weeping,
with no children to comfort them.

The station is now empty
and the mothers are wandering
through the dark streets of London.

Jennifer Morgan (12)
Carmel Technology College

THE CHILDREN'S WAR

At the start of a long, hard day,
Lots of hard work and no play,
Only the teacher knows where we're going
But really, there's no way of knowing.

When the children arrive at the station,
They wonder about their destination.
The chuffing steam train
Seems like a game,
But their lives will be held in slow motion.

Chuff, chuff, chuff, chuff,
Soon all the noisy rush
turned into a quiet hush.
No pulling, no push,
Then the children get on to the train
And wait for the 'hoot' again.

They sit in the train
Wearing a label with their name,
A gas mask hung in a box.
They carry their clothes and toys,
Lots of girls and little boys.
Very soon, they would get some awful shocks.

Some children had never seen
The green and leafy scene
Where they were to live for a while.
They waited patiently to be chosen by a family
And thought they would enjoy life in good style.

The children soon grew sad,
They missed their mums and dads
And wanted to return home more and more.
But they were made to stay
In the country far away,
To keep them from the horrors of war.

Elizabeth Steel (12)
Carmel Technology College

EVACUEES

Down at the station,
With a suitcase in one hand
And a gas mask in the other,
Unknown destination.

Frightened, cold and confused,
People are not amused
With mixed emotions
Caused by commotion.

The rattling rail,
Going slow as a snail.
The steaming train,
People feeling the strain.

On the train,
The food's so plain,
Lucky if you get some
Children missing their mums.

Off the train,
The station so plain,
People wrapped in brown,
People give me a frown.

Michael Collins (12)
Carmel Technology College

HERE WE GO

Here I am packing my bags,
Hurriedly, rushing till the clock strikes five.
Hurry, hurry it's time to go,
I'll miss the train if we don't hurry up.

The clock strikes five,
I'm saying goodbye.
The train is coming,
I'm beginning to cry.

I'm on the train,
Thinking what my destination will be,
While other children are weeping all around me.

My owners have led me to my home,
Where I'll be staying for a very long term.

I'm now in my comfy bed, going to sleep,
Thinking what my future will hold for me,
Wishing I was at home with my family.

Donna Varley (12)
Carmel Technology College

ACCIDENT

Riding on my bike, flying down a hill,
Enjoying the excitement, the fun, and especially the thrill,
Then in a flash, a moment, a crack,
I witnessed my brake cable snap.
Tragedy, hurtling towards a river bank,
All of a sudden, everything went blank.

Gary Johnson (13)
Carmel Technology College

SAY GOODBYE TO THE KIDS

Early one morning, the train
chuffed along the tracks,
whistling into the station.
The children piled on,
not knowing their destination.

The children are on, off goes the train.
The naughty children are being a pain.
At the end stop, the teacher says 'Off you pop,'
and each child hops off and begins to roam,
as each parent chooses a new lodger to take into their home.

The well-off adults pick the posh ones,
and the scruffy ones are left till last.
Along come the lonely adults
and whisk them off very fast.

The adults take them home,
the nice ones give them a bath.
Then they eat,
and have a good old laugh.

The children then sit down,
their pen and paper at the ready.
To write a letter home was their task.
Their pace was very steady.
They hoped that their life would get better soon,
but when you are an evacuee in life,
you will just have to wait and see.

Emily MacGregor (12)
Carmel Technology College

HERE WE GO!

It took me a while to pack my case,
I glanced at my mum, a frown on her face.
We walked off hand in hand
To the station of Bablegrand.

I stood small and scared at the station,
I wonder where will be my destination.
My mum gave me a loving look,
And for the journey, a picture book.

My eyes fill with tears,
The war soon nears.
I gave my mum a hug and a kiss,
My mum I know I would miss.

A man grabbed me and threw me on,
I sat on a seat made for one.
I waved to my mum out of the window,
As the train chugged on with a steady flow.

I saw some fields filled with sheep
And piles of hay laid in a heap.
The train chugged, chuff, huff, puff,
This whole time for me is gonna be tough.

We were the first to stop,
I jumped off with a hop.
This man shouted out my name,
To the others, he did the same.

I'd never thought much about home.
Anyway, where was I? Rome?
I pictured my mum all on her own,
Will she survive alone?

'I'll have her' someone screamed,
This man was rather nice it seemed.
We walked off hand in hand,
To the town of Castlerand!

Danielle Stott (13)
Carmel Technology College

AN EVACUEE'S POEM

To the station we all trooped,
in a great big, huddled group
Only the teacher knowing
the place to which we were going.

When the train arrived,
everyone piled on,
some children saying 'Don't worry Mam,
it won't be long.'

The train started up with
a loud, roaring noise,
which drowned out the sobbing
of loud girls and boys.

We arrived at the station
with a few clues of our destination.
Off the train we all rushed,
to find out who was looking after us.

I'm happy here at my new home,
missing my mum because she's all alone.
I know someday I'll be back
to see her, and my black cat.

Kaylee Scaife (13)
Carmel Technology College

WHY ME?

I stood at the station,
Waiting for my destination,
Thinking about my old home
Will my mum be all right alone?

The train came by,
People started to cry.
We all piled in,
Our heads began to spin.

The train went off in a rush,
We all sat in a hush.
Noisily it chuffed down
And out, out of the town.

The wind started to blow,
The train started to slow.
I looked around,
There was no sound.

We all got off the train,
Stepped out into the rain,
Walked along, side by side,
Some ran off to hide.

I was about to meet my new family,
I felt all confused and scrawny.
Was I going to be happy,
Or was I going to be lonely?

No one knew.

Sarah Smith (12)
Carmel Technology College

KENNINGS 'DOLPHINS'

An intelligent mammal,
A kind friend,
A gentle sleeper,
A fun-loving creature,
A nosediving expert,
An ocean lover,
A deep diver,
An endangered species,
A fish eater,
A great listener,
For everyone to love.

Danielle Cammock (12)
Easington Community School

KENNINGS 'DOG'

A furry friend
A heavy sleeper
A fun-loving creature
A cat catcher
A ferocious growler
A bone hider
A faithful companion
An intelligent helper
A personal bodyguard and burglar alarm
A man's best friend.

Helen Alp (12)
Easington Community School

EASINGTON GROUNDS

Droplets of rain hang from rooftops waiting in
exhilaration for their departure.

Telephone posts stand proud as they hold the
topic of conversation.

The grass has a grey complexion as it reflects
off the gloomy sky above.

Wooden fences and creaking gates stand in a row
like dominoes, each one cloning the next.

Sheets of ice lie flat and mischievous
as they plague the ground.

Young mothers trundle miserably up and down the
street with their prams of young children.

Unwanted litter is a constant visitor of the land.

Raised voices shout angrily above one another
while the audience watch at their doorstep.

The street lamps still emit a
glimmer of hope on the new day.

Nikki Foster (14)
Easington Community School

NIGHTLIFE IN THE STREET

Day is ending, sky is dark and stars are bright. The wind howls and drifts forcefully down the now emptying street.

Street lights are illuminated and flicker repetitively, spreading light throughout the sheet of black now covering us.

A group of children playing and laughing are parted by the echo from calls of their parents. Disappointedly they disappear.

A car passes over the gritty, uneven roads spraying a cloud of dust and pebbles into the air.

By now, shadows have fallen. Silhouettes of white outline mysterious objects, casting an eerie atmosphere everywhere.

The wind bites, scattering a mass of litter through the chilled air, which falls to the floor like a pattern before rearranging and lying lifelessly once again.

Trees also make silhouettes and the leaves shudder in the strong breeze. Their branches swaying and rattling, losing leaves which cascade to the floor.

A stray dog explores the litter in desperate hope for food, but discovering nothing's there, scatters off hurriedly.

Looking across the rooftops, empty and dark. The street is peaceful, air now calm.

So as the lights from surrounding houses go out - the day is gone and all that remains are dreams for tomorrow.

Helen Smith (14)
Easington Community School

MY STREET

Sprawling fields lay across the ground,
like a patchwork quilt, blanketing small animals.

Beyond them lies weeds tufting out from a spoiled hospital,
memories ruined, what secrets lie beneath?

A canvas for children provides shelter from the rain,
as elderly seekers wait for a bus.

Across the road stands a box for letters,
leaves cross its path as the wind swirls them in all directions.

Zigzagged wooden fences rise and fall with each slope of the grass
the droplets descend and seep into the lined grain.

Wood pigeons fly from tree to tree and circle the pergola
which now stands bare, stripped of its jewels.

The winding path of steps sinks deep into the dene,
the canopy of leaves no longer keeps out light.

Towering over slabbed stone drives, metal gates are set,
their black colour contrasts with the sky.

Wired, wooden poles stand transmitting conversations,
in a line, neatly placed in the grass.

A milk truck parked in a yard watches the splashes
of water beat down in the light of its beams.

Jennifer Styles (14)
Easington Community School

SUNSET ON THE AVENUE

You stand at the beginning and see fields,
Corn waving in the breeze and horses grazing.

Idly, ignoring inhabitants of the street as they pass
In their self-centred, private worlds - adults, youngsters.

Grandparents and children talk happily as together they stroll
Past cramped houses, curiously peering at neighbour's yards.

Fingers scrape along separating walls, pulling ancient mortar
From between the jagged bricks, avoiding the scrambling feet

Of carefree, playing children. A dog stirs restlessly, tied to
His kennel, nestling comfortably in a corner; he longs

To join the straying dogs walking the streets
As lions roam the Savannah. They growl at passers-by.

A stereo crackles into life and sound booms around the houses.

The deafening noise attracts complaints and drowns conversations,
But the listening teenagers increase the volume.

Filled dustbins mournfully sit waiting
For their contents to be wrenched from them while

Graffitied lamp posts line the pavement, impatiently longing
To light the streets with imitation sunlight.

The sun lingers an extra minute, hanging in the sky

Before dipping below the golden horizon, signalling
The end of the day, and the start of the future.

Vicky Maddison (14)
Easington Community School

Autumn Evenings

Tired people returning from a hard day's work
Parking their cars against a cracked curb.

More cars pull over,
Creating a rainbow of colour.

Weeds brushing against rubber tyres
Battered by the cold autumn wind.

Trees lean to one side,
As if listening.

The wind howls through the guttering,
Sounding like a restless immortal rising from its grave

As it pushes clouds drawing over the street
Like a sombre cloak trying to cover us with its eerie darkness.

No more people roam the street,
A chill is in the air.

The street lamps blink on
Casting fiery pools of light

Across the pavement and into
Empty blocks of yards.

A stray ball rolls down the street
Bouncing on loose pebbles.

Silence hangs in the air.

The only thing moving is the wind.

Windows radiate a warm glow
Protecting the families inside

As outside, there is nothing
Until summer comes round again.

Raindrops hang on telegraph wires
Like a string of twinkling stars

Looking like a glimmer of hope
For the bleak months advancing upon us.

Kirsty Golden (14)
Easington Community School

HARMONY ON HALLFIELD DRIVE

A stream of soapy water travelled down the street
While a man stood admiring his freshly washed pride and joy.

A small display of rubbish littered the worn tarmac footpaths
Bushes trailed on them shedding their tiny branches.

Lavender and small white flowers along with large sandy stones
Surrounded the street's freshly painted sign.

A good attempt to make the street seem greater than it could
Ever be.

Large brick walls and painted steel gates enclose the grave-filled
Burial ground. Even the fresh, colourful flowers failed to disguise
The grey shadow that the cemetery cast over the street.

Traditional chimneys, who were extinct, have been replaced by thin,
Grey pipes. A familiar scene emerged as a young child was beckoned to
come inside as darkness fell.

Alone, a street light flickered on and off as if being controlled by a
switch. Cold and bored children attempted to fit on the one grit bin as
others were settled inside for the long and nippy night.

Donna Weatherall (14)
Easington Community School

NIGHT LIGHT ON CLAPPERSGATE

Children send tyres spinning, over tarmac, down driveways
Eyes smiling, voices calling, feet pushing, riding

Past the smooth-haired prowler, heavily breathing as it buries
Its nose in the ground. Its padded paws

Softly stepping by tufts of grass seeping through
Slabs like bubbling lava, searching for the sunlight.

Reflected in the windows is the end of a rainbow.
Gold light streaming, dancing as it signals sunset. The day's end

Brings red bricks of bungalow aglow like a
heated iron. Welcoming, warming as children enter their homes.

Perched on wires evening music boxes tweet their chorus.
Heads bobbing, beaks calming ruffled feathers.

Hanging dishcloth in rags and tatters is a
Puppet for the wind to play with, flapping as the golden gleams retreat.

A solitary lamp post startles shadows.

New light is shed on rain which darts like arrows,
Shattering on contact with the ground's defensive shield, bouncing

Off collapsed guttering. Swarms of
Raindrops spurt free plunging into the unknown.

Beyond the towering tree tops a flag pole rises
Into darkness, from a smokeless blaze of silent fire, illuminating the
church, which the onslaught of raindrops fail to quench.

Elizabeth Long (14)
Easington Community School

WINDOW

Flowing fields of waving stems
Making up for the emptiness

Drenched wicker provides
Odd uneven mini-buildings.

The hedges distance themselves
For the fear of not being symmetrical

Over discoloured tiles of the greying barn
Where inspiration is lacking.

Tall spruce nod in unison
In the season of wispy breeze

Constantly trampled on, now grubby
Steps make an easy access

Leaves drop from the moulting branches
As crispiness falls to the dusky ground.

Mazes of block paving continue in
Meaningless patterns with an aim only to confuse as

Plywood messily strewn lies
Peacefully by the derelict barn.

Fuzzy images of unknown objects hide in the shadows
Not shown until domination has repositioned.

Stephanie Armstrong (15)
Easington Community School

My Street

Looking out of my bedroom window, I see my neighbours
Laughing, drinking round the smoking barbecue

It is noticed that the sheets hanging out to dry
Are being enveloped in the smoke

Hastily shoved in washing baskets the smoky sheets
Are carried inside by

Women wearing sun tops taking advantage of the sun
While men wash their cars

Parked lopsidedly in the driveways like frightened beetles
Their hard shells mirroring the sun

The children of the street play football
Using lifeless lamp posts as goal posts

Until they tire of that and fall asleep
Closing their eyes on the blinking lamp posts

Chintz cushions are brought from indoors to try to
Make the plastic garden furniture more bearable

But still they whine

When the sun settles behind the threatening-looking clouds
Blankets are produced

To warm the slurring adults against the night chill
But then they are too comfortable

And the soft conversation slowly drowns out
As one by one, they fall asleep.

Deborah Milburn (14)
Easington Community School

THE LOOKING GLASS

Black skies drape over the street
Street lights glimmer, casting aside the gloom.

Cool winds whip up shedding autumn leaves.
They glide softly like the crests of gentle waves
Through the crisp breeze.

Trees tower high, their armour
Bathing in silver rays.

Odd footsteps creep through the silence
Cutting through the stilled street.

A distant noise rumbles past
Gone, and the silence remains.

Wind lashes at doorways,
Invisible hands creak at rigid windows.

Old eyes have stared over the street
From the building down the road

Their identities unknown,
Nobody cares about the nursing home.

But over distant years, they've watched us all
From a looking glass from above.

We have never noticed that we are passengers of time
Growing old, we are oblivious
But not those eyes watching from
The looking glass down the road.

Gemma Hough (14)
Easington Community School

My Gran

My old gran is so nutty,
She stays up to watch the footie,
She plays games and fiddles with drains.

She's skinny and weedy and wears a pinny,
She loves baking cakes and making scones.

She loves a man called Drew and he likes a good brew.
Every day when he comes round, they walk
hand in hand to the bandstand in the park.

She loves me loads and loads,
But at the minute, she has a bad cold.

My old gran has now passed away
But every night, I cast a spell
Wishing her back to me.

Before she died she said to me
Look for the brightest star every night
And that will be me.

Samantha Richardson (13)
Easington Community School

There Are Lots Of People . . .

There are lots of people who bawl and shout!
You can hear them through walls and all about.
These people are really noisy, just like me!

There are lots of people who are really dumb,
When they hold a pen, their hand goes numb,
But me, no way, I work and work until my hand's sore,
Even though it is a bore.
These people are really not like me!

There are lots of people who love to sleep,
They only wake to the *beep, beep, beep!*
These people are really like me,
Because I love to sleep!

Kayleigh Rawlinson (14)
Easington Community School

NEW DAY, NEW SURPRISES

Winking, sugar grain stars
Dissolve, milky moonlight fades

Away, the night tied with a sunny bow
As the day brings fresh surprises.

Foamy clouds linger, like marshmallows
And cheery red cars top nutty pavements

Sticky-nosed folk, sealed in boxed homes
peek from behind candy-shaded curtains

Looking for action, drama, goings on
In a mild, hushed street

A single lamp post, bubblegum stained when unlit,
Beams fruit glazed light in full glow.

Minty green grassland, like patchwork
Surrounds households, chimneys puffing thick liquorice smoke.

Like a box of chocolates,
Assorted people, different centres,
Some bitter, some hard, some soft.
The street, compact, but full of treats.

Chloe Shaw (14)
Easington Community School

SUMMER STREET

A burst of light emerges as a glowing ball appears
And casts a golden blanket on the rooftops as the day awakes.

Blistering heat encircles contented children
Dancing on trampled grass.

Parents soak up sun, sprawled sluggishly
On vibrant deckchairs.

Mongrel dogs scour streets seeking sanctuary
In cool shade.

Parched soil grasps spraying water
As it pours constantly from hoses.

Music floods the area rapidly
Ghetto Blasters perform from house to house endlessly.

Echoes of laughter are heard
Parties reach their climax.

Barbecue smoke clouds humid air.

Sun gleams fade into distance
Golden blanket becomes a tide of dusky shadows.

Summer days conclude as light dims,
Crimson sky sets, street sleeps.

Ashley Hutton (14)
Easington Community School

MY GRANDMA MARY

My old grandma was called Mary
She lived in a street where she was quite weary

Grandma's favourite spot was in her chair
Rocking and brushing her long, wispy hair

She was only thin and very small
She had a carer incase of a fall

She loved to bake a good chocolate cake
Set on the table for children to take

She loved me and I loved her
She liked to be warm, wrapped up in fur

Never would she go anywhere alone
If she wanted to go somewhere she would give me a phone

My grandma let me sit upon her knee
She knitted jumpers just for me

If ever there was a problem we needed to share
She had told us that she would be there

Grandma loved jewellery earrings and pearls
She played with my hair and took out the curls

Being with my grandma sure made me smile
I will always keep her photos safe in a file

My grandma Mary soon passed away
But she has told me always to say

Look into the sky for the brightest star
And if ever you need me you know I'm not far.

Faye Boyle (13)
Easington Community School

MY GRANDMOTHER

I have a grandmother who sits in her chair,
Next to a brown, cuddly teddy bear.
She has very short hair,
It is the colour grey,
She will sit there all day.
On a night she will pray
About another day.

When my grandfather was here
They used to walk along Seaham Pier.
She told me that the sea was clear.
Her house is quite small,
Her windows are quite tall,
She can often hear my grandfather call.
Last week, she had a nasty fall.

She often talks to her friends about me.
I'm quite small, but not as small as you can be.
She sometimes gets me mixed up with my sister Claire,
When I sleep at her house, she says take care.
She can't drive,
But she likes to jive,
My uncle is called Clive.

She likes drawing flowers,
She can draw for hours.
She likes to dance,
Read books about romance.
She has a friend called Jean
Who is nice, not mean,
She makes me laugh and scream.

Janine Colwill (13)
Easington Community School

MY GRANDAD

My grandad loved keeping fit,
He never really liked to sit.
He played football, he played cricket
And took it badly when he lost his wicket.

When he was not very busy,
He acted very silly.
He wore my grandma's clothes
And soaked us with the hose.

He watched the football the other day
And told me off for being in the way.
He wouldn't move from the telly all night,
And wouldn't notice if I was in a fight.

On a Sunday, everyone's boring
And most grandads are usually snoring,
But not my grandad, he's playing cricket
And trying hard not to lose his wicket.

My grandad loved me and I loved him,
He was fit, but became awfully slim,
Then we found out he was dying
And everybody couldn't stop crying.

He gradually became sicker,
And also became much thinner,
He missed playing football, he missed playing cricket
And bought me a football ticket.

He passed away soon after,
Much to everyone's disaster.
Now he's gone, I play cricket,
And I take it badly if I lose my wicket.

Kym Nugent (14)
Easington Community School

First Day At School

Easington Comp is amongst the best,
All the pupils are soon put to the test,
When you first arrive at school,
You are soon abiding rules.

Your form teacher is the one
To pour out your troubles on.
She will help you settle in,
Being there, encouraging.

Finding classes is a chore,
Being late just once more.
At the sound of the bell,
Wondering what tale to tell.

When it comes to dinnertime,
You will have to stand in line
Wondering what you will say,
Pointing out your meal today.

Going through the big, wide door,
Wondering which corridor,
Feeling down and pretty low
Until someone points the way to go.

Sitting here an hour or so,
Waiting for the bell to go.
My first day has gone so well,
Never thought I'd live to tell
All about the things I've done,
Joining in, having fun!

Walking to the awaiting bus,
Wondering at all the fuss
I'd made about my first day at school,
Now I know it's so cool.
All new starters listen here,
There is absolutely nothing to fear!

Dale Roberts (12)
Easington Community School

MY POEM

As he comes you see him.
Wouldn't want to be him.
Bullies. I hate those.

Nothing you can beat
Tastes so very sweet.
Sweets. I love those.

Nobody is buying,
People sitting and crying.
War. I hate that.

Some sound like boats,
Fluttering with notes.
Music. I love that.

Don't drop your tins,
Put them in the bins.
Litter. I hate that.

Brings you so much glory,
Takes you to the story.
Books. I love those.

Faye Thompson (13)
Easington Community School

Colour Poem

Black is loneliness
With no one around,
Black is shivering
Like a child on a winter's day,
Black is your inner hole
Only you know it's there,
Black is unloved
An orphan on its own.
Black is diseases
Spread in poor worlds,
Black is a baby's mind
Until sight of our world,
Black is a widow
With no one to cherish,
Black is the war
Something there is no need for,
Black is empty
Hollow inside,
Black is heartless
With no one to love or care,
Black is a deserted town
Empty houses and shops,
Black is a lonely man's destiny
All bottled up inside,
Black is in a cold graveyard
With graffitied gravestones,
Black is non-existent
No life at all,
Black is here to hold up the stars
When we are asleep.

Karen Bainbridge (12)
Easington Community School

I'm Your Friend If You're Mine

I'm an angel
You are my friend,
I hope you are with me from the beginning to the end.
I will always be here for you through the good times and the bad,
I hope you will be with me when I'm sad.
You are my friend and I am yours,
We shall stay friends from the beginning until the end.
Friends are there if you need them,
Never choose your partner over them,
For they will come and go but friends are always going to be with you.
So choose your friends wisely,
And just remember if they are there for you,
Be there for them too.

Karl Davis (14)
Easington Community School

The Boy On His Bike

He was playing on his bike,
The dainty little trike,
Racing along the dirty path.
He will definitely need a bath.
Smash he went, over the wall,
He landed on a cricket ball.
Crack went his poorly leg,
He then met a nurse called Meg.

Michael Lee (11)
Fyndoune Community College

MOON

Dark,
But it's bright
During the night,
The light that I love
Shone long on my bed,
Don't blink
Or you'll miss it,
And it may not come back.
Your chance that you had,
Gone in a day, to be awoken by
New light just as bright,
But not as beautiful.
Butterfly silhouette
Upon my window net
The wings are dark,
But the moon makes them glow.
I know you fell in love,
From looking above through your window.

Paul Rowland (16)
Fyndoune Community College

LONELINESS

Loneliness is like a single flower in a vase,
Like a woman in a hall of men,
Like a daisy in a field of roses,
Or like a dog in a field of cats.

Loneliness is like a tiny fish in a sea of great white sharks,
Like the first tooth in a baby's mouth,
Or like a pretty shell in a bucket full of sand.

Deborah Jewell (13)
Greenfield Comprehensive School

AN ALIEN VIEW OF THE WORLD '99

Is the world-wide web
where a giant spider catches
a little fly?
Is the Internet a
fishing rod
to catch a fish
and make a pie?
Is cyber space
really on the moon?
The millennium will be here soon.

To surf the web, might I get wet?
Does jelly always have to set?
Why do lemonade bubbles go up your nose?
Why not up your arm, or
through your toes?
Why is Macauly Culkin
always home alone?
What is a Millennium Dome?

I'm a Martian boy
from plant Mars.
We have no buses, trains or cars,
restaurants, clubs or wine bars.
We fly around in spaceships
watching the human race,
but I wouldn't want to live on Earth.
I'd rather live in space!

Sabrina Parker (13)
Greenfield Comprehensive School

BONFIRE NIGHT

A whistle, a bang, a flare,
That's the rocket way up there.
A whoosh, a spin, a squeal,
That's the brightly coloured Catherine wheel.
A bang, a hiss, a crack,
That's the fearsome little Jumping Jack.

Cascades of colour way up high
Brighten the November sky.
A fire burning bright and hot,
Don't forget the Guy on top.
Children and adults gaze in delight,
On this cold November night.

We're hungry, we need something hot to eat,
Potatoes from the fire are a tasty treat.
Something else to keep out the chill,
A hot mug of tasty beef Bovril?
Oh yes, it sure is a night to remember,
It is, of course, the 5th of November.

Shannon Peacock (13)
Greenfield Comprehensive School

THE WRITER OF THIS POEM

The writer of this poem
is as tall as a house,
as quiet as a mouse,
and is as slow as a louse.

As gentle as a lamb,
as pretty as a picture,
as sweet as strawberry jam,
and as tasty as cake mixture.

As smooth as silk,
as chirpy as a bird,
as pure as fresh milk,
and as yellow as lemon curd.

The writer of this poem
never ceases to amaze,
she's one in a million billion,
or so the poem says.

Lynsey Bailey (13)
Greenfield Comprehensive School

SILENCE

Silence, whispered words.
Thoughts not speech.
Open mouths, no talk.
Time ticks, ears strain.
No sound, incredible pain.
I can be your mouth
But I cannot speak your thoughts.
What would you say?
How do you sound?
Nudged into the dark.
Ignored by the outer world.
If only you could love me,
I could come out of the dark.
I could speak of my devotion to you.
That will never happen though,
So I will just go on thinking in
Silence.

Craig Taylor (13)
Greenfield Comprehensive School

THE DRAGON

Underneath the churchyard far away from sight,
is a bloodthirsty dragon waiting to give you a fright.
He flies over Darlington with nothing much to do,
but before you say he's nasty, let's listen to his point of view.

I fly over Darlington looking at all the shops,
watching where I'm going, not to bump into building tops,
making sure I don't knock over the church steeple,
while listening to screaming people.

Sometimes my tummy gets rumbly,
and it's just because I'm a bit hungry,
then I dive and eat a McDonald's shop.
Start again, trying not to stop.

Anna Drury (11)
Greenfield Comprehensive School

CATS

Cats can be big, cats can be small,
cats can be cute, but not them all!
There's the panther, cheetah, leopard an' all,
bloomy me, there's more than three,
we sold them all to the junglerey!
I wonder if we can buy them back,
but yet again there's the house cat.
These have not been sold to the . . .
take a guess, it's the junglerey.
You can't take the jungle out of the cat,
but yet again, we never think about that,
the angel cat.

Claire Brown (11)
Greenfield Comprehensive School

TARA THE TERROR

I have a little dog,
Tara is her name,
Running after cats
Is her favourite game.

She's small and rather hairy,
And my brother thinks she's scary.
She always bites him on the hand,
Which I think is rather grand.

Oh when her teeth flash,
They could make Superman dash.
She sleeps on the couch, not in her box
And I think she resembles a fox.

She has a beautiful mane,
And sometimes she's a real pain.
Oh Tara, Tara, I really love you,
But sometimes, I think you belong in a zoo.

Emma-Jane Robinson (12)
Greenfield Comprehensive School

THE SEA

The sea is raging, like an angry tiger.
Be careful as the waves come higher,
Foaming, like a wild dog's mouth,
Careful! It's coming closer.

The light is now turning dark,
Waves crashing, like the jaws of a shark,
Covering up all the sand and shells.
Careful! It's coming closer.

Lisa Robinson (12)
Greenfield Comprehensive School

BULLIES

Bullies are people who laugh and stare,
Bullies are people who pull your hair.

Bullies are people who stare and shout,
To make you sad so you have doubt.

Bullies are the people who stare and shout,
If you tell, it will be sorted out.

Bullies are people who make you feel
All alone, like you've got no friends,
Like you're on your own.

Bullies are people who twist your arm,
Money they demand, you've done no harm.

Bullies are people who want to be found,
Unless you tell, and stand your ground.

Kayleigh Harle (13)
Greenfield Comprehensive School

THE EAGLE

Swooping, soaring in the clouds,
Flying round the mountains proud,
Never will he be cowed.

Flying up so very high,
Swiftly does the eagle fly,
Stark against the azure sky.

Victoria Wilson (12)
Greenfield Comprehensive School

THE ORPHAN

I sat there alone
on my bed,
wondering if I would
be fed.

My shirt was scruffy,
my jeans were torn,
sometimes I wished
I hadn't been born.

My parents died
when I was younger,
so I was an orphan
who starved with hunger.

The orphanage maids
were not kind,
so I thought about
leaving the world behind.

When supper came,
I took my knife
and within a few seconds,
I surrendered my life.

Now up in heaven,
I can see
there are people with
worse lives than me.

Katy Miller (13)
Greenfield Comprehensive School

THE PEST

Billy is my brother,
He's nearly three years old.
I love him like no other
But my story must be told.

He looks just like an angel,
With short blonde curly hair,
But don't be fooled by his good looks,
You really should beware.

He'll make you think he's oh so good,
With his lovely big brown eyes,
But it must be understood
He's a demon in disguise.

He gets into my bedroom
And turns it upside down,
He loves to break my precious things,
He really goes to town.

He kicks the dog and makes him growl,
Throws things at my TV
And when mum asks him 'Who did that?'
He says, 'It wasn't me.'

He gets me into trouble,
And then I get depressed.
I know he is my brother,
But to me he is *The Pest!*

Lucy Bradley (11)
Greenfield Comprehensive School

ME AND MY GUITAR

Strum, strum, strumming,
Tap my feet and humming,
With my rock guitar,
Music blasting afar.

Amps are bursting with the sound,
Rock and roll goes round and round,
Plectrum, strings are on the move,
Boys and girls they love to groove.

Rhythm, lead and bass with strings,
Hear the vocalist when he sings,
Drummer drumming to the beat,
A brilliant feeling with the heat.

Andrew Richardson (12)
Greenfield Comprehensive School

CAT

I am the cat that chases the bird,
All my friends think I am quite absurd.

I am the cat that catches the mouse
As it returns to its little house.

I am the cat that laps the milk,
Or the cream, smooth as silk.

I am the cat that gobbles my food,
Daintily from my own little bowl.

I am the cat that sits on your knee
Purring away contentedly.

Catherine Bell (11)
Greenfield Comprehensive School

SONNET SUFFERING POEM - CRAZY LIFE

All over the country every morning there's screams
Spots and bad hair should never been seen.
When things only ever go right in your dreams
It makes you see you should never be too overkeen.
The day I've been waiting for has finally come
The boy of my dreams asking me out.
I can't believe it, my knickers are up my bum!
I knew it would never go right tonight.
Oh no my trousers have split
What can I do, it's all gone wrong?
I have to go home and stitch it
But then I won't know if he wrote me a song.
All I'm left with is a hole in my trousers and no one to love.
My life is like a singing dove.

Donna Austin (13)
Hurworth Comprehensive School

THE BLUE SEA

The blue sea sparkling in the sun,
Screams and laughter,
Sound of children having fun,
The sand gently washed
By the crest of a wave,
The water creeps into
The deep, dark cave,
The green seaweed slowly sways
Beneath the surface of the sea,
Everybody's playing in the water
Full of happiness and glee.

Stephen Tremewan (11)
Hurworth Comprehensive School

PAIN

Pain:

It hurts so bad,
The injury,
The thoughts.

Pain:

Knowing people are dying,
Knowing people are fighting.

Pain:

Seeing things you don't want to see,
Hearing things you don't want to hear.

Pain:

You can't escape,
It's there all the time,
So you might as well get used to it.

Kelly Pybus (14)
Hurworth Comprehensive School

AUTUMN

The leaves are falling slowly but surely,
The frost is creeping up on us.
The days are shorter by the week,
The weather turns wetter and colder.
Winter slowly sets in,
Bonfire night is here.
The sun filters out to a flicker,
Autumn is here in all its glory.

Jonathan Roche (11)
Hurworth Comprehensive School

THAT'S LIFE

Bullies and baddies never cease,
And so the hurt and the pain won't go away.
It's like your clothes when they're creased,
And the embarrassment is there to stay.
The experience of love can hurt,
And friendships can just die.
There's times when you feel like dirt,
And when nothing goes right, why?
You can suffer emotionally,
This is when you're sad and crying.
Another way is physically,
It's when you've hurt yourself or you're dying.
Mentally's the last one, that's a torturous thing,
All these ways and more, are part of suffering.

Alison Galpin (13)
Hurworth Comprehensive School

A DAY AT THE BEACH

The sun is rising in the sky,
And the moon is going to say goodbye.
The sea is turning a nice pale-blue,
The birds are beautiful, singing too.
The tourists are coming out to play,
They're hoping it's a summer day.
The sea is methodically brushing the shore,
And the wind has started to blow more and more.
Today it has been really bright,
But the day is slowly turning into night.
The people are going and saying goodbye,
And the black darkness of the night creeps like a sigh.

William John Harrison (11)
Hurworth Comprehensive School

MY FRIEND (THAT'S GONE)

I looked out of my window,
I saw your face,
You said you would never go
You left me your love, just in case.
You were my best friend,
You were always there for me,
Then all of a sudden, your life came to an end
The justice in that, I just can't see.
The drugs were what did it, you couldn't stop from the start.
I will never forget your face that day,
You're still in heart.
Your life just wasted away.

I'll say goodbye never
In my heart you will live on forever.

Emma Graham (13)
Hurworth Comprehensive School

THE WAVES

The powerful waves hit the sandy beach
Like a stone hitting the ground
The waves hit with such might
The rocky mountains start to crumble at their feet
Only few can withstand the might of the waves
And of all that tried only few succeeded
And the rest have been forgotten.

Evan Smith (11)
Hurworth Comprehensive School

OH NO!

Oh no! I looked in the mirror,
There's a spot on the end of my nose.
My T-zone has a glistening shimmer,
And my face is a pale shade of rose.
My hair is a mess,
It just won't go right,
I wish it was a bit less,
I think I'll hibernate 'til night.
Slap on some make-up,
Extremely quick,
Cover that spot up,
With a concealer stick.
After all that I look in the mirror,
The spot has gone and there's no glistening shimmer.

Toni Elizabeth Leach (13)
Hurworth Comprehensive School

HOT AIR BALLOON

Up, up away in my hot air balloon
High up, the trees grow small.
Blue sky above my head
Fluffy clouds at my feet.

The flames as they roar
Fill my balloon.
The birds as they sing
Fill my ears.

Up, up away in my hot air balloon
High up, the world below is quiet.
Green fields far below
Blue sea in the distance.

Samantha Oates
Hurworth Comprehensive School

AN ICY WINTER

My favourite season is winter,
The ice and the snow.
I feel a chill down my back,
Wherever I go.

White fluffy balls are falling,
The ground is white.
The trees are bare,
Not a leaf in sight.

A shriek of excitement,
A great atmosphere.
Christmas is arriving,
Santa is here.

Lauren Robinson (12)
Hurworth Comprehensive School

BEING UNLUCKY

When you sleep in,
When you walk out the gate,
And realise that you are late,
Then you slip on a banana skin.
The lottery I thought I'd win,
I got the ticket in too late,
I should have had it in by eight,
So I threw my ticket in the bin.
My homework is due in tomorrow,
I didn't remember 'til half-past nine,
My dad was blind drunk on wine.
My heart was filled with sorrow,
Life today is such a bummer,
I may as well just do a runner.

Steven Wilson (14)
Hurworth Comprehensive School

SUFFERING

On a dark and lonely night,
My mind was playing tricks.
On that dark and lonely night,
My brain was in a mix.
Because there it was standing,
By the open door,
Reaching its hand in,
Wanting more.
Wanting more blood
From the veins in my neck.
Then it bites, the blood rushes in a flood.
It stops to check,
To check to see,
If he has done his duty.

Nichola Ingledew (13)
Hurworth Comprehensive School

SUNSET ISLAND

Sunset Island is the place to be.
Sunset Island is the place for me.
With forests and mountains and a village to see,
It really is the place to be.

The sun shines brightly upon the sea.
So come and take a swim with me.
Watersport Beach and Paradise Bay,
Are two places you can lay.

Cally Jameson (11)
Hurworth Comprehensive School

SO THIN AND WORN

She's over there
She would snap so easily.
Sat in the chair
Her legs swinging so weakly.
If you look at her face
So thin and worn.
She's just sat in a daze
Waiting for the bell, there, it's just gone!
Runs down to lunch to get thinner,
Then to the bathroom,
Down the toilet she throws up more than her dinner
Next she's lying in a hospital bed full of gloom,
She's just laying there crying,
Laying there practically dying.

Kayleigh Evans (13)
Hurworth Comprehensive School

FALL, TO FALL

Teetering on the edge,
A multitude of thoughts in my head.
Should I?
But what will I be leaving behind?
I smile.
Then I fall
And I'm falling
Falling. Faster.
Waiting for the inevitable.
The mandatory sickening thud.
But it never arrives.
Perhaps I'll be falling forever.

Laura Bernstone (15)
Hurworth Comprehensive School

THE ABANDONED BEAR

I am an abandoned bear,
Sitting alone on a shelf.
I used to have someone who cared,
But now I'm all by myself.
All my children have grown up and gone
Leaving me all on my own
I used to have friends, but now I have none,
Just a silent and lonely home.
Moths are eating away at my stuffing,
Slowly I'm fading away.
Very soon I'll be reduced to nothing,
I won't see another day.
If only all the children could see,
How much love they could give to me.

Jennie Haines (13)
Hurworth Comprehensive School

A MONSTER POEM

In the night the monsters awake
With slimy jaws and a tongue like a snake.
Bulging eyes and spiky blue hair
And eyebrows like bushes.
It will make you stare.
The light comes on, the monsters hide
And when I look they're gone.

Michael Lawson (11)
Hurworth Comprehensive School

LOVE

There they are walking down the street,
Fingers entwined, hand in hand,
Through the scorching, blazing heat,
Down the road in lovers' land.

Parting is such sweet sorrow,
He touches her face, they dance, she's so excited.
They can't wait 'til tomorrow,
He looked at her, she was what his heart demanded.

She arrives home her smile full of joy,
He arrives home, his eyes full of fire.
He is all she thinks about, her lover boy,
She is all he thinks about, his messiah.

Their love is strong and even stronger,
They will be together for long and even longer.

Katy Williamson (13)
Hurworth Comprehensive School

THE SUN

On the never-ending horizon with boats passing by,
I could see the orangey sun falling gently from the sky.
I asked people scurrying around
Why the sun sinks into the ground.
This as an answer nobody knew
Will I ever find a person with even a clue?
To give me the answer, that's all I ask,
The answer to my never-ending task.

Tanya Atkinson (11)
Hurworth Comprehensive School

SURVIVING SPROUTS AND TROUTS

I sit and eat my vegetables,
Gulping down my sprouts.
I feel like I'm unable,
To put one more in my mouth!

My appetite reduced to nil,
As I start on a serving of trout.
Now I'm beginning to feel over-full,
No energy to scream or shout!

Not much more to go now,
And Mum's gone for a minute.
She's back, she looks and then she says,
'But how did you manage to finish?'

So remember children if you're eating trouts and sprouts,
Keep a bag handy to secretly throw them out!

Laura Todd (13)
Hurworth Comprehensive School

AUTUMN AND SUMMER GONE

Autumn comes, summer goes
Coloured leaves drop from trees
Weather changes throughout the days
It starts to rain, so we can't play.

Hayley Waters (11)
Hurworth Comprehensive School

FOOLS FALL IN

I have a sad story,
That I would like to tell,
But it is quite long,
And I am not well.

One day I went climbing,
God knows why,
I broke my right arm,
And fractured my thigh.

Last week I went skating,
On ice in fact,
I fell over and went flying,
My skull is now cracked.

Last year I learnt to wrestle,
But that wasn't a good idea,
'Cause the guy jumped on my back,
And he nearly broke my rear.

Tennis was my favourite sport,
Until a few days ago,
She hit the ball very low,
And now I've broken my toe.

That's my story right to the end,
I'm really full of sin,
So now remember in your brain,
That fools always fall in.

Laura Evans (12)
Hurworth Comprehensive School

THE FAIR

The wheel is spinning round and round
20 feet off the ground.
It goes around in circles
The spinning colours blue and purple.

The twisters spin from side to side,
It gets so scary you try to hide.
You get on just for the thrill but when you get off
You feel rather ill.

The pirate ship goes very high up
And down side to side.
It takes you high it takes you low
You feel like you want to go.

Round and round the waltzers go
Spinning fast away we go.
The most fun day I've ever had
To leave the gates was so sad.
In time left I have to spare
I'll be back to see the fair.

Sarah Newrick (12)
Hurworth Comprehensive School

SUFFERING

Suffering is like that horrible night
Of falling off that bike.
With that enormous, large fright,
That you really don't like.

Once upon a time, I had a smash,
Which hurt an awful lot,
As my legs had a large crash,
With the base of an old rusty pot.

I had a split-open knee,
So as loud as I could, I shouted for help.
And within minutes, three
People heard me yelp.

I was sent off to a hospital ward,
I fully recovered,
But without my bike I'm totally bored.

Peter Hedley (13)
Hurworth Comprehensive School

THOUGHTS

The damp, grey beach is clear,
The air is cool.
Walking to rid *fear,*
As the day draws in.

                    Long dark caves,
                    They are getting deeper.
                    Rock-*smashing* waves,
                    Pulverising into little pieces.

The harsh silence,
What's it going to teach?
All ongoing *violence*
When's it going to stop?

                    These little voices screaming,
                    Why, I don't know.
                    There isn't any meaning,
                    It will never *stop.*

Danielle Ratti (12)
Hurworth Comprehensive School

SCHOOL

School, school what a stupid rule,
You can't not go because the law will know.
Nagging teachers, parents too,
This is what they say to you:
Don't run,
Don't chew.
Doing this won't be fun.
Do your homework, do it right.
You can go out tonight.
School, school, what a stupid rule
You can't not go, because the law will know.
Rules, consequences and rewards,
This is what schools use most.
You're late!
Listen to me!
The rules are here, look and see!
Formal warning,
White slip.
In detention.
I'm sick of this.
Well done!
Red star!
Certificate of merit.
You'll go far.
School, school, what a stupid rule,
You can't not go, because the law will know.

Fern Holmes (12)
Hurworth Comprehensive School

HALLOWE'EN

Hallowe'en's the time for scary fun,
Kids all dressed up, frightening everyone.

Kids running around with bags of sweets,
Knocking on doors, 'Trick or treat'.

Carved pumpkins with creepy faces,
Bats and spiders found in all places.

Cauldrons and hats, broomsticks and witches,
Magic spells and potions for itches.

Stories of werewolves, monsters and ghosts,
These are the things that scare people the most.

These things are also fun at Hallowe'en,
Most of them make people *scream!*

Katherine Hodgson (12)
Hurworth Comprehensive School

JUST CONTEMPLATING

I am standing at the top of the abyss
contemplating whether to push myself in
the people I thought I knew are now distant strangers
I contemplate the easy way out
I hear a voice, I hear a shout
it calls my name over and over
I turn to see the face behind the voice
As I turn the feelings glow
I remember the good times and the bad
but as I think the memories flow
and into the abyss I will go.
Will people remember me? I don't think so.

James Humphreys (16)
Hurworth Comprehensive School

TRENCHES

The lone soldier lies dying in his bunk,
His arm severed by an enemy grenade,
Slowly draining his body of his blood,
The battle rages on.
Guns blaze slowly chopping holes in the German defences,
Leaving hundreds to die in the cold embrace of no-man's-land.
As the blood seeps into the mud of the battleground,
The millions not wounded in battle, slowly decaying from lack of
Fresh water and malnutrition.
Awaiting the final order to clamber out of the trenches in an attempt
To destroy the Germans.
But slowly the guns die down as the remembrance of all who lay down
Their lives to protect their loved ones.
Poppies from in-between the mud and blood
As the final reminder of the horror and suffering of the *world war*.

Daniel Robinson (13)
Hurworth Comprehensive School

LUCY THE DOG

I thought I was a loveable dog,
But it seems not to be,
I was thrown out into the fog,
With no one but me.
What a nice home I'd had,
With my soft cosy bed,
I must have done something wrong,
As for days I wasn't fed.

I wish I could go back,
And finally get dog food to eat.
Maybe one tin, or perhaps a pack,
Or even just a piece of meat.
I wanna go home,
I wish I could go home.

Stuart Lowis (13)
Hurworth Comprehensive School

THE ISLAND

There is a special island,
That I would love to visit,
It has everything I want,
It matches me like a dream.
The climate there is so warm,
I wish I could try it,
Get away from wet old Britain,
And come back with a tan.
The people are so friendly,
They always have time for you,
Giving advice showing the way,
Making it a nice holiday.
It sounds like such a perfect place,
So tell me, can I go?

Oliver Welch (12)
Hurworth Comprehensive School

WHAT'S THE POINT?

What's the point in life and all its simple rewards?
What's the point in anything, anything at all?

What's the point in marriage, temporary happiness?
What's the point in being born, a temporary quest?

What's the point in learning for our future?
Why oh why?

What's the point in working towards retirement?
Why do we try?

What's the point in smiling and trying to be pleasant?
Is it our duty or perhaps our destiny?

What can I myself achieve, in my short existence?
A cure for hunger and suffering, can I make a difference?

What's the point in friendship and all the woes it brings?
What's the point in love and trying to live like kings?

Remember this simple fact, pleasure leads to pain.
Is anything worthwhile, what can we gain?

Think about it, just for a second
What's the point in anything, anything at all?
Then the answer hits you . . . everything.

Andrew Bernstone (12)
Hurworth Comprehensive School

TEN HAPPY SCHOOLGIRLS

Ten happy schoolgirls all went out to dine
One ate a bone and then there were nine

        Nine happy schoolgirls went out very late
        One got found out and then there were eight

Eight happy schoolgirls sailed down to Devon
One went overboard and then there were seven

        Seven happy schoolgirls each had a Twix
        One had 57 then there were six

Six happy schoolgirls were dancing to the jive
One slipped over and then there were five

        Five happy schoolgirls went to watch a show
        One forgot her ticket and then there were
        four

Four happy schoolgirls got chased by a bee
One got stung and then there were three

        Three happy schoolgirls all had the flu
        One got a blocked nose and then there
        were two

Two happy schoolgirls singing a song
One lost her voice and then there was one

        One sad schoolgirl all on her own
        Sat down on the fire, then their was none.

Jennifer Tremewan (12)
Hurworth Comprehensive School

Annoying Brother

My brother is annoying he is like . . .

An itch in the middle of your back you can't scratch.
A bottle of ketchup when the ketchup won't come out.
A pen that won't write.
A car that won't start.
A really long queue,
A thing that you want to buy being sold out.
A baby that won't stop crying.
An awful TV programme.
A broken toy.
A load of homework.
A bad hair day.
An embarrassing parent.
A big test.
And a nagging grandmum.

My brother is very annoying.

David Parsons (12)
Hurworth Comprehensive School

Winter Is Coming

Winter is coming soon
Chilly nights all the time
Winter, winter is coming.

Buying Christmas trees
Presents too
Winter, winter is coming.

Trees are bare
With no leaves
Winter, winter is coming.

The nights get colder
Darker too
Winter, winter is coming.

Snow is falling
Everywhere
Winter, winter is here!

Harry Knott (11)
Hurworth Comprehensive School

THE PONY IN THE PADDOCK

Chestnut brown with golden mane,
Small and Shetland, seems quite tame.
Looks at me with big round eyes,
Trots to me and sniffs my thighs.

He always comes when I call,
I tack him up, saddle and all.
Around the paddock we like to ride,
Jumping poles with one big stride.

We do diagonals, walk and trot,
Working hard and getting hot.
We go from trot down to walk,
Then pet my pony, have a talk.

To the stables we have to go,
Plait his tail, put in a bow.
Groom him with his grooming brush,
This is the part we must not rush.

In the stable my pony does stay,
Munching on bales of golden hay.
The time has come to go to bed,
Close your eyes and rest your head.

Rachael Doubleday (11)
Hurworth Comprehensive School

FOOTBALL

Football
The greatest sport ever
Better than all the others
More shooting
Football

Football
The greatest sport ever
Faster than all the others
More shouting
Football

Football
The greatest sport ever
More amazing than all the others
More suspense
Football

Football
The greatest sport ever
Bigger than all the others
More running
Football

Football
The greatest sport ever
Funnier than all the others
More energy
Football.

Jonathan Dees (12)
Hurworth Comprehensive School

A Winter's Walk

Slight traces on winter trees,
As the plants and flowers start to freeze.

        Pearl-white sheets of pocketed snow,
        Leaves brown, Christmas pudding,
        Soil glow.

The crystal panes of river ice,
Thick enough to roll a dice.

        Filled with clear water, underneath,
        With moonlight that lights its darkness
        From its sheath.

Echoes of distant sheep in a herd,
And distant chirps overhead from a bird.

        The gusty gales carry a winter's breeze,
        Carrying the dead, crispy leaves.

The dark grey clouds form in the sky,
As the hooting owls fly along by.

        The light flaky flakes of frost,
        Cover the door's footsteps that are lost.

The churches clock strikes at midnight,
As the sky falls, too dark for sight.

        A walk here on a cold winter's night,
        Is risky for fear of frostbite.

Gemma Coverdale (12)
Hurworth Comprehensive School

ISLANDS

I stand alone.
Unbridged waters divide us all.
Only the loudest cries carry across,
The brightest light.
Not close enough to notice the features.
Untamed tides that cannot be conquered,
Hammering our shores.
Even those bridges that are built
Can be destroyed.
Some say it's true
That only one bridge remains.
But for some,
No bridges are built strong enough.
At times it seems those closest to me
Notice least,
Looking too close to see the full image.
Will I always wonder
If I can cross the water?

Chris Devlin (15)
Hurworth Comprehensive School

POEM OF MY BODY

I don't like to stand around
You'll often find me sitting down
My legs go weak and buckle
That would cause me awful trouble.

I do like to run quite fast
But don't mind if others pass
My heart beats like a drum
By now my lungs have gone quite numb.

At night I find it hard to think
My brain goes dead in a wink
I think for now I'll put it away
And keep it for another day.

Sarah June Johnston (12)
Hurworth Comprehensive School

TABLE TENNIS

Play it for a sport
Or play it just for fun
Play it in the rain
Or play it in the sun

Play it with a bat
Play it with a ball
Smash it really hard
And bounce it off the wall

Give a backspin serve
And make him hit the net
Win another point
And then you'll win the set

Play it in your garden
Play it in the street
Play it with the vicar
And everyone you meet

When you get tired
Don't sit in sorrow
Go and have a sleep
And play again tomorrow.

Andrew Leighton (12)
Hurworth Comprehensive School

SPORT

The gun blasts
The race lasts
No time at all
The cheering crowd
Is very loud
Though the pace is a crawl

The whistle blows
The ball flows
Without a single hitch
In no time at all
The striker has the ball
And is away off down the pitch

The favourite serves
And he deserves
To win the tennis game
He is very fit
Shown by his hit
He will get all the fame

Her finest dive
She will survive
Though the board is very high
A backflip
With a twisted hip
Is the last dive she will try.

Alex Moore (12)
Hurworth Comprehensive School

BRAVE BOYS

Sombre nights, only the rats as company
Your best friend is face down in the mud
Corroded lungs left to rot
Entangled in the enemy barb
Only the eerie glare of the green flares to guide you
Guide you to an almost certain death.

'Come on lads,' says the sergeant trying to lift morale
But he knows the horror that awaits us
The fate which had been met by other 'brave men'
Or as it is 'brave boys'.

By the time of the attack, men were shell shocked
Some were already dead
The others were terrified and those scared the most
Those who were desperate
They found that they had somehow been shot
But still, they weren't the lucky ones
Brave boys.

The time had come
Our time was up
I could not think how noble it would be to die for my country
But I could only think and despise the generals
The Pompous men who put the death sentence over our heads
Brave boys.

Over the top
In a wave of green tunics
Which soon became red, as each man fell
Some still alive, whose screams would haunt the next wave
But I was the lucky one, a shot to the head
Nothing! Brave boys!

Daniel McDowell (15)
Hurworth Comprehensive School

ON AN ISLAND

On an island,
far from home
where big and ugly
beasts do roam.

On an island,
far from home
where lonely creatures
sigh and groan.

On an island
far from home
where temples tower,
made of stone.

On an island
far from home
where the sea and I
sit alone.

Gemma Phillips (11)
Hurworth Comprehensive School

MY CAT, VESTA

I have a cat that has been rescued
He often comes for food and pesters me.

He mostly eats,
And then sleeps.

My cat's fur is black and shining
He has his own mat specially for dining.

My cat has sharp glistening claws
On his soft padded paws.

Now and again he goes and stalks
Just like a hunting hawk.

Once he came inside with a live mouse
And let it go into the house.

Sara Allan (11)
Hurworth Comprehensive School

AUTUMN DAYS

Autumn days shed warm glows of light,
That notify the animals it's time to sleep
The leaves all drop
Leaving a blanket of red, gold, brown and crimson.
When I walk through the park the leaves start flying,
Powered by me and the wind
The conkers all drop,
Leaving endless fun with conker matches.
The seeds all drop bringing new growth and life
And bring a year full of food,
The sunset sun
Projects beautiful reds and gold.
Then after autumn the leaves start to grow
And the cycle starts again.

Lee Weeks (11)
Hurworth Comprehensive School

PARADISE ISLAND

As the dazzling sun shines from above,
giving light to Earth
its glittering powerful rays send light
to life below.
Through the wild river life you have
never imagined before.
With exotic fish, echoing valleys.
Golden beaches with tiny pure grains of sand
which have the special silky touch.

The cloudless, blue, tinted sky,
a vast sheet covering the exotic land,
the towering peaks of mountains overlooking
the tropical fruits ripened
by the kindness of the sun.
The humming of the birds so soft
so calm, so peaceful.
The thick mist silently covers the mysterious
wondrous life hidden deep inside.
The rainforest's life may be hidden but,
the sound is never hidden and never will be!

But this luxurious island has not only tourists,
hotels and amusements
this island is full of life, natural places
but it is still, calm, relaxing and living.

Shahnaz Romeela Rana-Rahman (11)
Hurworth Comprehensive School

THINK IT THE HAPPY WAY

The shopping mall,
The sweetie stalls,
The frosty snow,
I like that stuff.

The mellow sun,
The swiftly moving sand,
I love teenage love,
When your heart tingles,
For the very first time,
I love that stuff.

But then I hate the way,
Your heart breaks,
Your whole body self seeks,
But can't find any attention,
I hate that stuff.

I hate the way the snow melts down,
Like a life drifting away,
I hate that stuff,
Especially when you're so near,
And a voice cries out but you cannot hear,
A hand pulls them in,
But you can't pull them back out,
I hate that stuff.

I hate the way we visit their graves,
And mourn their bodies,
But as the summer light comes through,
Their souls are up there waiting for you,
I love that thought.

Sacha Marie Buckley (13)
Hurworth Comprehensive School

MY HANDSOME PRINCE

I thought my life was over,
Then I wondered what to say,
I knew my handsome prince would come some day,
I sat there on my own,
Wondering when he would come,
I thought my life was over.

He turned up on my doorstep,
I wondered what to say,
He gave me a quick smile,
I knew my life remained but
I thought my life was over.

'My name is Prince Derek,' he said,
I knew I should tell him mine.
'My name is Claire,' I replied.
I knew my life remained.

'Do you know the way to York?'
I didn't know what to say.
'Come in for tea,' I said 'and I'll tell you which way.'
I thought my life was over.

I told him which way,
He went during the day, I thought he was mine,
I knew my life was over.

He turned up on my doorstep,
I knew he'd come back to me,
He was here for me.
I knew my life remained.

He wanted me to marry him,
How could I resist?'
My love had finally come,

I knew my life remained.

Claire Reese (12)
Hurworth Comprehensive School

I KNOW WHAT IT'S LIKE

I know what it's like when you feel down
I know what it's like when no one's around
To heal your pain or make you smile
Or to talk to you like it's worth their while.

I know what it's like to feel lonely and sad
I know what it's like when people make you feel bad
When you've done nothing wrong except say to them
That you wish you could do it all over again.

I know what it's like to feel left out
I know what it's like when no one's about
For you to talk to about what you're feeling inside
Then they try not to show the boredom inside.

I know what it's like when people say 'No.'
I know what it's like when people say 'I know
What it's like' when they don't have a clue
But I know what it's like I honestly do.

Emma Todd (15)
Hurworth Comprehensive School

LAKE JANJIRO

Lake Janjiro in the morning sun,
Glistening like the blue ocean on a sunny day,
I look across the shimmering lake,
I see the dense rainforest,
With birds sleeping happily in the trees,
All is still.

I look across the lake once more,
I see the shadows of the trees dancing on the water,
The reeds and grass,
Covered in gleaming morning frost,
Melting in the rising sun.

I must go now,
For soon the animals will wake,
Then there will be silence no more.

Sophie Oldridge (11)
Hurworth Comprehensive School

DOLPHINS

I am a big blue dolphin
I roam around the sea
I love my name which begins with 'd'

I am a big blue dolphin
With all my chatty friends
We all sleep in our dens

I am a big blue dolphin
I can eat a ton of fish
And that's a secondary dish

I am a big blue dolphin
It's time for my bed
Well that's what Mummy said.

Gemma Wilson (12)
Hurworth Comprehensive School

NAPALM ATTACK

The sounds of death destroyed the night air.
Overhead, in the dark, smoky sky,
the B-52s moved silently,
searching.
The trees in the forest were all stripped bare.
The leaves ruined,
destroyed.
The unmistakable odour of Agent Orange clung to the poisoned bark,
yet still, there were no sounds to be heard.
The Vietnamese were cowering,
frightened,
terrified of the American tormentors who were taking away their
existence.
They weren't ashamed to hide,
but the Americans were ashamed of themselves.
How had it come to this?
Was this the price to pay for others thinking in a different way?
The napalm fell like black rain,
drenching people with its lethal shower,
and still they refused to give in -
all of them.

Nicola Foster (15)
Hurworth Comprehensive School

A Part Of Me, Gone

When he left I waved to him.
His smiling face just visible, from the window of the train.
And he waved back,
His young, smooth hand
Just distinguishable in a sea of others.

When he had gone I wandered home.
I didn't think for a minute
That he would never return.
I never imagined that I would not wave him into the station
Just as I had waved him out.

I didn't toss and turn in our bed
Wondering if he would ever lie next to me again.
My mind did not run in anguish
Imagining some terrible fate for him.

When he died I was there,
Created by his fading thoughts
His young, desperate eyes, turning
In haunted sockets to meet me.
I held his bony withered hand
Gently, as if it were of the greatest value in the world.

When he left me, I turned away.
His disfigured face, just visible
In a mass of others.
His wasted body, leaking its life
Into a running stream.

And a part of me went with it,
Turning, leaping and bubbling down.
Sucking life, youth, hope and dreams
Down, to Earth.

Rozi Smith (15)
Hurworth Comprehensive School

FIREWORKS

Gold to pink then to green,
Some of the fireworks that I've seen,
Dazzling sparks fill the air,
So make sure you take care.

Fireworks shoot up into the night
As the bonfire is set alight,
Children's faces show no fear,
As the fireworks disappear.

In the sky there is a glow,
As the bonfire burns below,
The image of Guy Fawkes burns bright,
On the dark November night.

Children marvel at the sight,
Whilst cats and dogs get a fright,
Fireworks are nice to see,
But they say to you *don't* mess with me.

James Chapman (11)
Hurworth Comprehensive School

Lost

I'm lost far away from my home,
Rough out on the back street.
I sleep on a small piece of foam,
And I'm dirty right down to my feet.
I have not eaten in days,
I search for scraps in the bins.
If only I could change my ways,
Maybe some fish in tins.
The night is silent, all is dead,
I ache, I am all worn.
I need a night's sleep in my bed,
I have only one eye, my leg is torn.
Then one day came a girl named Claire,
She saved me from this terrible nightmare.

Amy Sedgwick (13)
Hurworth Comprehensive School

The Millennium

I woke up bright and cheerful,
My heart was like a singing bird,
Whose nest is in a watered shoot.

Thinking what will the future hold for us people?
Who knows?

Will we drive automatic cars?
And will everything be more advanced than before?
Who knows?

Will people's lives change,
Or will people move house just for the millennium?

Nokkaew Harrington (14)
Hurworth House School

FUTURE

As I enter this space age time,
Starships zip by
On a super highway.
A shadowy man passes me,
And an eerie chill envelops my mind,
A silky butterfly.
I slither along the street,
Floating on my feet.
A battle fleet of tyrant hybrids
Glide down from the sky
And deliver their fiery wrath.

Daniel P Hall (13)
Hurworth House School

THE FUTURE!

Whoosh! Whoosh!
Spaceships flying everywhere
funny looking things that people wear.
Bleep! Bleep!
Robots working all around
reappearing underground.
Zogbo! Zogbo!
Aliens ruling here and there
playing jokes on people's hair.
The future is dark and still
The people there have to kill!

Stephen Looney (12)
Hurworth House School

BEYOND

Beyond the grey and gloom of life,
Is where many cases lie,
Of crimson veil,
And woeful tale.

The twisted voice of expectation calls,
Of one's own truth or lies,
Yet the drab voice of reality fades,
Can this be my beyond?

And know this,
Truth or lie,
You cannot hide from your truth,
Your beyond!

Ben Harrison (13)
Hurworth House School

FUTURE POEM

S pace is a place that's vast and wide
P luto is just an hour's ride
A nother galaxy has been found
C reatures there do abound
E veryone makes a different sound.

John Harland (13)
Hurworth House School

Millennium!

M ajor day, an
I nternational way with
L oads of people and
L ots of fun
E ntertainment for everyone.
N obody sleeps, everybody speaks.
N oise goes on
I nto the night
U ntil the clock strikes,
M illennium.

Ramesh Pani (11)
Hurworth House School

Things

Hovering, floating, suspended in the air,
red ones, blue ones, blazing everywhere,
left, right, and centre as they dodge through the air,
one shot right past me and gave me quite a scare,
my jaw hung right open, my eyes fixed with amazement,
as I just stood there on my dusty old pavement,
let's just hope for the future at least,
that these strange creatures mean peace.

Fergus Dent (12)
Hurworth House School

WAR

Clash of the swords,
Boom of guns.
Rolling of the tanks,
Roar of the jets.

Reinforcements are no good,
Like they are a sacrifice.
Only the strong survive in the savage game,
The weak flee like woman and children.
Everyone feels as if they will die,
Please let it be a dream, please, please.

Anthony Scott (12)
Hurworth House School

THE FUTURE

Simple shapes and empty rooms
Streamlined cars without the fumes.

Silver, chrome and gleaming gold
Modern shapes and perspex moulds.

Will we have more leisure soon,
Live on Mars and see the moon?

The future is another day
Not so very far away.

Alex Strachan (13)
Hurworth House School

Millennium

Voices make friends and unite us.
Voices make enemies and divide us.
Voices bring hope and cheer.
Voices bring happiness and fear.

People's voices loud and clear,
Across the land for all to hear,
Millennium 2000 year is drawing near.

Children's voices happy and light,
Singing loudly with all their might,
Bringing joy and peace by day and night.

Guy Severs (11)
Hurworth House School

Voices Of The Future

In the year 2000,
There will be space travel and people living on the moon,
With hovercars and transportation tubes,
Holidays for 6 months of the year.

In the future we will travel deep into space.
I will live in a house on the moon,
Built on the man in the moon's face.
When will this be! It can't be too soon.

Alexander Gardner (11)
Hurworth House School

IN THE FUTURE - I WISH!

In the future I wish
For intelligence great.
Then there would be no school,
As my brain scale would be first rate.

In the future I would like,
For long queues no more.
Just walk in, buy my goods
And walk back out the door.

In the future I hope for
All money problems to be solved.
With no more money needed
Everyone's lives would be resolved.

In the future I wish,
Oh I wish in my grave,
For gas central heating
To keep winter chills at bay.

David Burningham (10)
Hurworth House School

THE END

See the world of tomorrow.
See the grey dusty desert floors and smog-covered skies.
See the dead ruined cities and the wrecked streets.
See the old rusty war machines and the cold dead soldiers' graves.
See the bones of the people and their ashes in the air.
See the darkness.
See the end.

Scott Prior (14)
Hurworth House School

I Have A Dream...

I have a dream that the world will be peaceful
and it won't matter if the weather's bright or dull.

I have a dream that I'll find true love
and that in the skies there will be doves.

I have a dream that there's equal rights for everyone
and that countries will join up as one.

I have a dream that the world will be fair
and that everyone can have good health care.

I have a dream that skin colour won't matter
and no one will dress in rags and tatters.

I have a dream that war'll be no more
and people won't have to be poor.

I have a dream that the world is a safe place
and all children can safely play chase.

I have a dream that together we'll make
a world which is a much better place.

Joanne Smith (13)
Moorside Community School

I Had A Dream

I had a dream
that stars and moons
had faces on them,
so they could smile
at you when you
look up at them.

Claire Tilney (11)
Moorside Community School

I Have A Dream

I have a dream that on New Year's Eve 1999
everyone will celebrate in style as they take part
in a once in a lifetime experience.

I have a dream that all violence will end
in Northern Ireland, that all people will finally
end the feud that has ripped Ireland apart for many years.

I have a dream, that when I'm older I will
get a good job and support my family,
and that I will always have my friends.

I have a dream that violence will never again
happen at a football match. And that the players,
from both teams will get along.

I have a dream that Newcastle United will
start to play well again, like they did during the
Keegan era, and bring some trophies to their loyal fans.

I have a dream that from now on
all times will be good for everyone,
and we will never again have to revisit the bad times.

Philip Stephenson (15)
Moorside Community School

I Have A Dream

I have a dream
to stop world hunger
to stop the babies crying
to stop the children.

I have a dream
where there is food for everyone
and nobody is thirsty,
plenty of water to wash in
so no one is dirty.

Liam Galloway (11)
Moorside Community School

MILLENNIUM ARMAGEDDON

January first in the hands of fate.
January first, an infamous date.
A meteor heading for the earth,
The end is here or maybe the birth.
All hope is on the armed forces' elite,
From this life-sucking comet from which there is no retreat.

The worlds' nations all unite
Against the meteor for this momentous fight.
The enormous rock takes the bombs blow by blow,
But reluctant to move, it keeps its evil flow.
The day of judgement is now and here,
All hopes and prayers now turmoil and fear.

Armageddon is felt by all,
The human race awaits its fall.
Fixed upon the global killer are my eyes,
Six billion questions of ifs, buts, and mainly whys.
Reading this is a treasured find
For these are the thoughts that travelled through my mind.

Mark Turner (16)
Moorside Community School

NEVER

I had a dream that Mr King's speech comes true.
He had a dream, now I have one too.
I dreamt of a world where the past was altered
the Bayeux Tapestry wasn't thought of,
the Domesday Book never written,
Christopher Columbus never found America,
Samuel Johnson didn't know the meaning of all words
and
Isaac Newton was never sitting under the tree.
Would it make a difference if
Only nine states signed the Declaration of Independence
and
Abraham Darby erected his cast iron bridge over the River Tyne?
What if
Charles Babbage never invented the computer
The motor car was never invented
and
The Wright brothers never thought about flying?
What would happen if
Emmeline Pankhurst sat back and let only men vote
or if
Adolf Hitler was never born?
Would it make a change if
television wasn't invented
if Concorde never flew her maiden voyage
and
Neil Armstrong never reached the moon?
The millennium has brought these thoughts home to me,
we have had success, disaster, improvements and pain
in this millennium.

Let's see what the next will bring.
Millennium stands for the future,
time of perfect peace on Earth.
Now, let's see that in action.

Kimberley Kirsopp
Moorside Community School

I HAVE A DREAM . . .

I have a dream, and it's in sight,
and it will happen at midnight.

Forget about all those tears,
where have they gone, all those years,
lift your glasses, give a cheer,
fill yourself with the beer.

This bug they say,
will ruin the day,
but we will fix it by the New Year.

A long look back at good and bad,
some had happy, some had sad.

Glowing like shining silver,
let's see what 2000 will deliver.

12 midnight the clocks will chime,
the world is waiting. 'It is time.'

Friends and families all together
peace and joy and love forever.

The part has gone,
the future's come, let's party at the millennium.

Shauna Haley (15)
Moorside Community School

THAT OLD HOUSE

That old house,
That house up there,
I've been told
I am in for a scare.

Zombies, bats, spiders,
Dracula's lair,
I've been told
They all live there.

The wind howls,
And the moon is bright,
I am all alone,
At that house at night.

Trembling with fear,
I open the door,
I may meet death
When I touch this floor.

A shadow passes,
Could it be true?
Has Dracula seen me?
Oh no! It is true.

Closer, closer,
He comes
My heart is beating
Like a drum.

I fall to the ground,
I close my eyes,
Open them
Not a sound.

Where he went,
I could not ask,
But there before me,
'Twas like a mask.

Did I dream it?
I'll never know,
I'll go back to sleep now,
Very, very slow.

Katie Little (12)
Moorside Community School

VAMPIRE

I am a vampire,
the creepiest ever seen
I bite loads of necks to keep my teeth clean.
I always go out at the witching hour,
and always find my victims in less than an hour,
but if there's no one around in the dead of night
I must return to my coffin before sunlight.
I am a handsome man who wears a cloak and hat
and to escape people I change into a bat.
You can't see me in a mirror,
my reflection does not show,
I could be beside you right now,
and you would not even know.
The only thing to stop me from biting you again
would be to wear a crucifix
upon a chain.

Marc Gaines (12)
Moorside Community School

I Have A Dream

I n the future I would like to see,

H appy things, new things, things that haven't happened before.
A nother thing would be space travel,
V enus and Mercury would be visited,
E ven Pluto and Uranus would be in our grasp.

A ll problems with employment will be gone.

D ifferences between countries will be settled,
R acism and sexism will be ruled out,
E very Third World country will be equal to the rest,
A nd all suffering will disperse.
M aybe humankind will learn.

Andrew Williamson (11)
Moorside Community School

I Had A Dream

I have a dream of being a soldier,
serving the country,
shooting the enemy.
Throwing bombs in the barracks,
paratrooping into deserted areas.
Driving tanks,
escorting allied troops to safety,
and going home to my family,
I would hope to have a sparkling medal of honour,
I would like to fly around the world.

David Brewis (14)
Moorside Community School

IMAGES

I ntentions and creations,

H appiness and belief,
A mbitions, and creativity,
V iolence and peace,
E vil and goodness,

A rrivals and delays,

D ifferences of opinion,
R eality and disbelief,
E xcitement and joy,
A dventure and found treasure
M arriage and death,

F riends are forever,
O pportunity knocks,
R elationships fade,

T houghts and memories,
H aven awaits.
E periments of the future.

M ystical illusions
I magination and images,
L ove and disillusion,
L ife and the living,
E ternity unfolds,
N ow is the time,
N ew dreams become roles
I mportance is all dashed,
U nrepentant sinners,
M y millennium is a blast from the past.

Laura Kennyford (15)
Moorside Community School

MILLENNIUM

We're both called Laura and we just can't wait,
To welcome the new century with our mates.
We're going to have a party and go berserk,
But when the clock strikes 12 o'clock nothing's going to work!

It happened many years ago, 2000 to be exact,
A very special babe was born and this is a fact.
Jesus was His name and healing was His game,
Being the Son of God was His call to fame.

The Bible tells the story of Jesus and His life,
His parables and miracles and never-ending strife
His life cut short upon the Cross,
His death to the world was such a loss!

Since then many events have taken place,
And this is plain to see,
Romans, Vikings, numerous kings and queens
Are now part of our history.

So many things have happened in such a short time,
Wars, flood, famine, poverty and crime.
Rockets and spaceships and around the world balloons,
And don't forget Neil Armstrong who landed on the moon.

On the 31st December in 1999,
We'll drink a toast to Jesus with champagne and wine.
We'll welcome the millennium and have a really good time,
We'll all join hands together and sing to *Auld Lang Syne*.

Laura Brown & Laura Collingwood (15)
Moorside Community School

I Have A Dream

Year 2000
For some people a happy time
A new year, a new millennium
A reason to party and celebrate
With friends and family
Having fun,
Enjoying the exciting occasion.

Year 2000
For others, it's just like any other year
Another year of worry and sleepless nights,
Wondering whether they'll be able to afford food
Or find clean water.
Wondering what the next day is going to bring,
Whether war is going to strike,
Or if it's going to end.

Year 2000
Will it bring good changes to the world?
Will there be enough food and water to supply everyone?
Will there be world peace?
Or will people still suffer from hunger?
And will the wars continue?
I have a dream that there will be world peace
And enough of everything for everyone.

Pamela Butterfield (16)
Moorside Community School

MILLENNIUM DREAMS

The millennium is nearly here
mixed emotions, some excited,
others unaware and too young to care.
People planning parties to celebrate
but the new millennium
what will it bring?
Will everyone be treated equally?
Will the world be at peace?
Will we exist?
I have a dream
That the millennium
will bring peace and equal rights
more help for the homeless,
good health care for everyone.
I have a dream
that people will fulfil their ambitions,
that everyone is given a chance to achieve his goals,
that everyone is blind to the appearance of others.
The millennium is nearly here
mixed emotions and dreams.
The millennium
what will it bring?
Will everyone be treated equally?
Will the world be at peace?
Will we exist?

Laura Bean (15)
Moorside Community School

I Have A Dream

I have a dream that I hope will come true
In the year 2000 for me and for you
That the end of disease - famine and war
That the stopping of violence and a return of the law
Will all start to happen when the clocks start to chime
And peace and contentment will be yours and mine
Then Terry Wogan won't be on the tele
And Newcastle United give Man U some welly.
When I leave Moorside School with my GCSEs
And all the teachers go down on their knees
They bow their heads as we go through the gates
We're all joined together, we're friends and we're mates
Some will go on to great things and fame
And others do nowt, that's the name of the game
Some will get married and have loads of kids
Some will get drunk and end up on the skids
Others will go where the streets are paved with gold
And some will stay here and only grow old.
In the heat of the day and the cold of the night,
We'll argue our points whether they're wrong or right.
But one thing will join us wherever we be
Whether we're up in the air, on the land or the sea
When we were at school we all worked as a team
But we know that's not true, this is only a dream.

Victoria Bottle (15)
Moorside Community School

I Have A Dream . . .

Let us dream of a tomorrow,
Where our children are nourished,
Let our peace and harmony,
Show to everyone in our laughter.
Let us dream of dancing in the rain,
And let us renew once again,
The promise of harmony,
We all together made before.
Let us hold our heads up high,
Let us dream of a tomorrow,
Where our souls truly shine,
      I have a dream.

I have a dream,
That most agonising things,
Don't seem to be as confusing,
That the bashed, abusing victim within,
Is finally and kindly set free,
To honour our family and others,
To help the dying and lonely,
To comfort the homeless and hungry,
By caring for others and not ourselves,
'We'll make it better,' is their promise,
Why don't they do it?
      That is my dream.

Janine Collins (15)
Moorside Community School

I Had A Dream

I had a dream

Hope it comes true
Apples and cream
Doughnuts and brew.

A friend joined me in the eating

Dining together cream we were beating
Round and round till it formed a peak
Ending with arms oh so weak.
All of the meal was enjoyable
My oh my, it was certainly edible.

Nicola Price (11)
Moorside Community School

I Had A Dream

Chocolate, chocolate everywhere,
I walked through the door and stood
there and stared.
Oh, this is just too good to be true,
The chocolate factory is just new,
Across the road from where I live
So I had to go and say, 'Please give
some of that delicious chocolate to me,
white, dark, chocolate with cream.'
Then I woke up . . . I had a dream.

Louise Kay (11)
Moorside Community School

I Have A Dream

I have a dream that everyone in the world can have equal rights and live together in peace without violence and anger among many pointless wars that solve nothing.

I have a dream that people shall not judge people by their looks such as being racist and they should respect one another as we were all made to do.

I have a dream that we should use resources sparingly, not to be greedy and to share what others have not got and to make a change as we come into this new millennium.

I have a dream that people should not pollute the environment starting the new millennium in a mess, and there should be an end to crime and illegal drugs.

I have a dream . . .

Richard Chapman (13)
Moorside Community School

I Have A Dream

I have a dream
A dream that could come true
That all wars will stop
And that someone will come to help the poor
Through and through.
I always dream that everyone in the world
Will be happy forever.

Katie Lloyd (11)
Moorside Community School

WEMBLEY

I have a dream that my feet will grace
the turf of Wembley.
The same turf that Geoff Hurst graced as
he scored the winner at Wembley.
In 1966, the English cheered, the Germans cowered,
The greatest feet have graced this pitch,
Pelé, Gazza and Shearer.
But a shadow hangs over Wembley as they
are pulling the twin towers six feet under.
'Another stadium,' I heard them say.
'It won't be the same,' said my father and I.
The Germans will laugh, the English will cry,
It could make English football die.

Kieran Sharp (15)
Moorside Community School

I HAD A DREAM

I had a dream I could swim with whales,
They could tell me their thoughts and all of their tales,
About all the fishing boats that would come and go,
And all of the rubbish that would sink and float.
They say they are killer whales, but this I cannot see,
Because they are so friendly and very nice to me.
By the year 2000 you may not see,
Many of these black and white killer whales left in the sea,
So please save those whales, so in years to come,
They can pass on all of these tales to their young.

Donna Matthews (14)
Moorside Community School

BLAH, BLAH, BLAH . . .

I have a dream of this,
I have a dream of that,
Of a future of bliss,
With me, Poet Laureate.

No thanks, just joking,
But some fires need stoking.

The millennium is over-hyped,
While Third World debt, just won't be wiped,
We're spending money on useless monuments,
While some young children would kill for condiments.

Do I have a dream?
Is a dream worth dreaming
In a world of greed
With nothing as it's seeming?

No, but yes,
You don't get what I'm saying
Take a guess,
It's as relevant as my playing.

Can't you see,
Beyond the words,
Into my mind,
Into my world?

Richard Roe (16)
Moorside Community School

No Change

In the millennium the world will not change,
It will stay the same
Politicians will still be corrupt
It may be a painful pill to swallow
But these are the people we have to follow
I hope religion will be banned and then
Hopefully cultural differences can be spanned
Nothing will change
There still will be a very definite class range
The world will still be an open sewer
Spewing filth on the so-called worst
The very poor.
I have a dream it will change
I hope the monarchy will fall
And the judgmental pope will crawl.

Ritchie Rackham (16)
Moorside Community School

I Have A Dream

I have a dream
That the sun is shining
Brightly over fields of
Corn and rye.
It makes things grow
It makes people happy
It makes the birds sing a song.
It makes the stream sparkle
Like silver flowing coins.

Richard Walford (11)
Moorside Community School

I Have A Dream

I have a dream
Each night it's said
Whilst I am snuggled up in bed
This dream, it always makes me yell
A nightmare! As far as man can tell.
I toss and turn, I scream and shout
What on Earth is this all about?
Then all of a sudden, I start to sing,
I mutter something about the wing
My song begins to sound really loud
It must, there's such a giant crowd,
To my room dad rushes,
He asks what makes me scream.
I tell him not to worry,
It's my favourite football team.

Caroline Slater (11)
Moorside Community School

I Had A Dream

My dream was sort of funny
it was mapping my future out
I was up in space watching
the world wipe itself out.
It was kind of scary seeing
each country disappear.
No world to go back to
after the new millennium was here.

Helen Erving (11)
Moorside Community School

DAVID BOWIE

I   live amidst a world where

H omeless and sheltered
A nd destitution is sorted out
V aried taxes are no longer
E ducation has improved.

A narchy has matured

D isease will have been eradicated
R ight-wing radicals will have been stopped
E mpires will fall
A nd
M onarchies will cease.

F reedom reigns
O ver all
R ealistic ideas come into place.

M any lives will be saved and remembered
I   hope that prejudice has totally gone
L aw is upheld and
L aughing gnomes are in every garden
E nter the pragmatists
N o time for mistakes
N o time for prevarication
I   mages are less important
U nderneath is what's relevant but
M aybe I wish for too much.

Richard Flowers (15)
Moorside Community School

DREAMING

I have a dream that I will pass all of my exams.
I have a dream that one day I will see the world.
I have a dream that all of my fantasies will become reality.
One day, we'll all be treated equally,
One day we'll all get along.
In my dream, we were all together,
Singing together, dancing together, playing together,
And we were all free from disease.
There were no such things as murderers or rapists,
No sexists, no racists, no hatred or evil,
But kindness and love.
We all had human rights,
And there was no Third World,
No famine or war. Charity wouldn't be needed.
I have a dream that one day there will be world peace.
I have a dream that one day, dreams will come true.

Kim Brown (15)
Moorside Community School

I HAD A DREAM

I had a dream I went to Mars.
I went by rocket through the stars.
I met a Martian on that sphere,
Which made me scream and shake in fear.
I had a dream I was back on Earth,
No more Martians for what it's worth!

Benjamin Gibson (11)
Moorside Community School

THE CRYING ENVIRONMENT

I have a dream, no longer
Is there steam, now the uses
Of diesel, petrol and oil flow
In almost every stream,
No longer is the world clean.

Pollution on the ground,
Pollution in the ground,
Pollution is now all around,
No longer is the world sound.

There may be sizzling sun,
Though swelling rivers will
Burst their banks very soon.
Goldfish may be out of their tanks,
People will soon complain
Of having wet pants, when
Houses are flooded, all because
Of burst river banks.

Birds in the sky try to keep flying,
Fish now no longer worth frying,
Oil slicks in the sea,
Everything dying, soon it won't be
Worth no longer sighing, when will
People realise the environment is crying?

Paul Heatherington (15)
Moorside Community School

I Have A Dream

I have a dream where
Hopes all come true,
Ambitions fulfilled,
Nature treated right,
Violence is under control and
War and evil disappears.
Differences are settled,
Rape is unknown and
Illnesses all cured.
Everyone is equal and
Everyone lives in peace
No one is mistreated because
Man is kind.
The millennium, when dreams come true.
Up in the stars, I see peace.
I dream of seeing my grandad again,
I dream for excitement and to
Enjoy my life.
I dream for A's in exams
So I can be who I want to be.
I dream that friends are forever and
Love is true.
I dream that Newcastle is the best football team
And spiders are extinct!
The millennium, the party year, where
You can dream anything,
But in real life,
I dream, my dream comes true!

Gemma Symonds (15)
Moorside Community School

I Had A Dream

Half asleep,
as I lay in bed
don't know if it's real or not.

All night long

dreaming about bears
running after me,
each one getting closer.
A loud scream I give.
My mam then wakes me up.

Stacey Bell (11)
Moorside Community School

Under The Moonlight

Long, spooky shadows cast across the moist ground,
Red glow diminishes like a dying fire.
Blue horizon fades to black,
Moon illuminates the grassland like a torch in the sky,
Creatures emerge from dark holes in the earth.

Cunning foxes scrounge for food in the fields,
Wise owls patrol the air searching for prey below,
Bats screech as they pursue their supper,
Badgers rummage through the foliage of the forest floor.

Sky transforms to blue,
An orange glimmer sparkles on the horizon,
Moon disappears into the distance,
A new day dawns again.
Animals return to their homes,
They wait patiently for darkness to descend once more.

Sean Kay (13)
St John's School, Bishop Auckland

THE WAITING'S ALL OVER

On the grassy knoll
he sits, just waiting.
When the signal comes,
He'll let fire.
Bang!
One emission of tapered metal
Piercing the helpless body.
Cars motoring past,
Humming like a swarm of bees,
Highly agitated.
His nerves are fragile.
At any moment, he could
Slip over the edge of insanity.
The gesticulation comes.
The air is littered with
The sound of gunfire.
He strikes his target
With precise aim.
A roar, a chant,
He's won!
The paper target has been
Struck, directly through the heart.

Richard Morley (13)
St John's School, Bishop Auckland

WAR

Bloody fields, dirty trenches,
Tasteless food, awful stenches,
Explosions by day, gunshots by night,
How I hated to see the sight
Of soldiers I'd know who had been hit,
Trying to advance from the doom-filled pit.
They'd wait for a chance to fire up their gun,
But the sniper was there, that was it - done.

So many friends I had seen shot and fall,
Before they'd had chance to give it their all.
Firing and shooting was all I could hear,
I looked at my neighbour, his face frozen with fear.
I really felt I could take it no more,
I'd had my fair share of blood, guts and gore.
We'd try to keep cheerful talking of home,
Our hearts were despairing of what was to come.
But as I gazed round at the worn, tired faces,
At men living like animals in tiny, cramped spaces,
I knew we would bravely stand together or fall,
Bound tightly forever, all for one, one for all!

Katy Graham (13)
St John's School, Bishop Auckland

THE SKI SLOPE

The icy wind pinched hard upon my face,
  as I bent to make a laboured pace,
    preparing for my downhill race,
      my journey down the ski slope.

        I disembarked from button tow,
          to gaze upon the slope below,
            and concentrate upon the flow,
              of a journey down the ski slope.

            At summit, I prepared to slide,
              upon my very own gravity ride,
                as on the silvery snow I'd glide,
                  on a journey down the ski slope.

                Launched from the top, I realised,
                  and as I gazed was quite surprised,
                where I'd begun was quite a rise,
              on my journey down the ski slope.

            As I hurtled down the drop,
            My skis hit rock, I couldn't stop,
            I met the ground with skis on top,
          on a journey down the ski slope.

    And as I landed in a heap,
      in snowbank that was hardly deep,
  back to my skis I did quickly leap,
on my journey down the ski slope.

    At journey's end, I filled with cheer,
        for what at the top had been pure fear,
          had now changed into joy so dear.
            I'd journeyed down the ski slope!

Simon Temby (13)
St John's School, Bishop Auckland

TEENAGE TROUBLE

My life can be quite easy
If I forget my trouble,
I can relax and laze around,
But then my temper begins to flare and I begin to bubble.
It's hard being a teenager,
My head all full of stress!
Mum is shouting up the stairs,
'Your bedroom's still a mess.'

My life can be quite easy,
If I forget my trouble.
I sit, think, and ponder away,
Once again, I seem to be stressed, thoughts all in a muddle.

It's hard being a teenager,
My head all full of stress!
My hair's gone wrong,
My make-up's gone,
Where's my sister? Guess!

Mum says, 'Enjoy these special years
While you have got the chance.'
I don't see how, as half the time,
I'm walking in a trance!
My head all full of friends and school, clothes and
                              songs and stress,
Make-up missing, sister hissing,
And my bedroom's still a mess.

Penny Foster (13)
St John's School, Bishop Auckland

The Sea

As I watch the sea,
Crashing off the wall,
It gives me a deep feeling inside
Of happiness and contentment.
The waves smash into the rocks,
The spray ascends and we move away,
But it still manages to soak us.
I look out to sea and see white froth,
It reminds me of the foam in the bath.

The sea, for fish, is what they call home,
It gives them what they need.
They either swim in shoals or on their own,
It depends on their way of life.

The sea is wild
And it can be harsh,
It can even claim people's lives,
But then for some,
Like fishermen, it provides food and livelihood,
But at all times, should be treated with respect.

Michael Kirtley (13)
St John's School, Bishop Auckland

WHY?

Why can't we all be friends?
When will all this fighting end?
Why can't we all be friends?

Why can't people be nice and mild?
We're not animals, we're not wild.
Why can't people be nice and mild?

Why are we all at war?
Fighting's such a dreadful bore.
Why are we all at war?

Why are some people really mean?
They call us things like 'runner bean'.
Why are some people really mean?

Why isn't everybody nice?
They give me stares as cold as ice.
Why isn't everybody nice?

Why won't one tolerate another?
Some get hurt because of their colour.
Why won't one tolerate another?

Why isn't there peace in the world?
Let the flags of truce be unfurled.
Why isn't there peace in the world?

Rebecca Ferry (13)
St John's School, Bishop Auckland

DREAMING

As I jumped into bed, in the freezing cold night,
I looked out my window, the moon was so bright.
The stars sparkled in the dark black sky,
Whilst shooting stars twinkled, as they passed by.
Suddenly I fell asleep and began to dream,
Of all nice things like chocolate ice-cream.
But to my horror I heard a loud scream,
Not from the sky and not from my dream.
Slowly and gradually I opened my eyes,
I glared at the door and to my surprise,
There stood a small young girl,
Wearing a raggy white shirt, a torn black hat
And a long grey skirt.
I'd never been so scared in my life,
As a sharp shiver went through my spine,
She glanced at me then gazed at the time.
What was she doing? As she stared at the clock.
The time struck midnight and began to 'tick-tock'.
I watched with fascination, as she waved goodbye.
She jumped in the air, then started to fly.
She was gone in a flash,
And was nowhere to be seen,
So I slowly shut my eyes, and returned to my dream.

Casey Mangles (13)
St John's School, Bishop Auckland

THE APOCALYPSE

End of the world, you never would have thought
The day of reckoning was over.
Everything had vanished.
Yet it only seemed like yesterday
When I was dancing the fandango.

Flashes kept reappearing
Like the lights at a disco.
The rocks, blistering heat.
The meteor hit the earth
With a tremendous 'thud'.
The gas that it had brought was deadly!
My name was on a disc
That was around my neck: Freddy Smith.

How did I survive was the question?
The world used to be a wonderful sight.
Now it's just miles upon miles of red earth
As far as you can see.
Those were the days that we enjoyed
Before all of this catastrophe.

Carl McGregor (13)
St John's School, Bishop Auckland

FRIENDS

F riends are kind,
R eally caring,
I nseparable,
E nsure times together,
N ever give up,
D o things together,
S hare their belongings,
H elp each other through hard times,
I nsecure, when apart,
P eople who talk together.

W ill help me if I'm stuck,
I nside the group,
T hink of each other,
H old on to the friendship,
I nsecure when apart,
N ever leave me alone.

S tick up for each other,
C ome to lessons together,
H ope for us to do well in school,
O nly the insides count,
O pen up to each other,
L isten to what each other is saying.

Sara Elmes (13)
St John's School, Bishop Auckland

ON THE SPOT

You are in your first lesson,
Bored out of your brain,
You cannot wait until hometime,
Relaxing in front of the TV again.
The teacher asks a question,
And you do not have a clue.
You have not been listening,
So your brain is stuck like glue.
Mind begins to crumble,
Hands begin to shake,
What do you say,
Without making a mistake?
The victim feels a nudge,
Some paper has been passed,
Then in your moment of glory,
You shout out, 'He will not last.'
'So you were listening,' the teacher says,
And turns away with the twist of her head.
You let out a sigh of relief,
Then look to where she turns,
The next victim has been chosen,
But they know the answer because they learn.
I think I have learnt a lesson,
That I will never forget,
Next time I get my homework,
I will get it done before it's set!

Emma Haley (13)
St John's School, Bishop Auckland

Winter Wonderland

Silence
I listen, look and study
Why so quiet?
Dash to the windows
Pull open the curtains
'Yes,' I shout
The first snow has come
White wonderful winter
Little tiny birds' prints on the crispy layer
Two by two over the lawn
Like little train tracks.

Cars start to move very slowly
Crushing white ice beneath their wheels
I rush to get ready
Layer upon layer upon layer
Of winter woollies
Got to get outside before the sun
Comes glistening on the white carpet
Then all will be gone.

Michael Hartmann (13)
St John's School, Bishop Auckland

ANIMALS IN THE NIGHT

When the sun sets and night draws near,
Most of us are going to sleep,
But in the woodland,
Some animals are just waking up,
They have been asleep during the day,
And are searching for food at night.

Owls are nocturnal creatures,
They hunt for mice and other small animals,
When the owl spots its prey it swoops down,
Clutches it in its sharp talons,
To take it somewhere to devour it.

The shrew digs around in the soil,
Searching for insects and worms,
Making sure that it is not the next victim for the owl.

Then the shrew spots another owl flying closer and closer,
It runs for its burrow as the owl flies closer,
The owl gets ready to snatch the shrew,
Opening its sharp talons,
The owl reaches out for the shrew,
But the shrew reaches the entrance to its burrow,
And with a loud bang the owl crashes into a tree.

Robert Jones (13)
St John's School, Bishop Auckland

MY PETS

I have quite a few pets,
Seven to be precise,
But now caring for animals has become
Some sort of a hobby.
Just like other people collect models, cars or trains,
I choose to take in these seven animals,
But I still love them equally.

My hamster, named Albert, who is as fat as a pig,
Has a cage all to himself.
He nibbles away contentedly,
From his special bowl, which seems to hand it to him.
When he is sleeping,
His bed appears to cradle him, like a mother holding her baby.

As for my two dogs,
Labrador Lilly and Joe,
Lilly is the younger of the two and slowest.
As for energetic Joe, always on the go,
He's a Scottie dog you know.

I also have a cat named Tim,
A present for my birthday.
He likes to sleep, eat, drink, always with a slurp,
And sleep again, exactly in that order.

The remainder of the seven,
Are my three goldfish.
They all look very similar, so don't have any names.
But . . . that's all I'm allowed to have.
As my mum has now said 'No!'

Mark Henry (13)
St John's School, Bishop Auckland

SPACE

The vast desolate wasteland,
Ruling the skies with planets and stars.
During day, you cannot see
During night,
Its stars and planets
Light up Earth's majestic body.
Its constellations,
Give us beautiful pictures of ancient myths.
Zooming comets light the sky.
So beautiful, the thousand colours of its tail.
So dangerous it is to us.
The question is,
Is there extraterrestrial life out there?
Are they little green men, or are they blue?
Antennae with eyes on the summit.
Warp speed ships orbiting planets.
This is space,
The final frontier for all humanity.
Or is it?
Will men rule the vast void called space?

Philip Santana Smith (13)
St John's School, Bishop Auckland

WAR

Why do people go to war?
Some for money or land.
Some because of religion,
Some because of their colour.

Soldiers out on the battlefield,
That really want to be home,
Guns, loud bangs,
Screams of terrified people,
Relations wondering,
Will they see loved ones again?

War has stopped,
But thousands are dead.
Innocent people shot,
Courageous soldiers killed.

Why?
Why did so many have to die?
Why was so much blood shed?
Some try to hide from war,
They push it to the back of their minds.

Not all can forget,
People who lost loved ones,
Soldiers suffering,
Will constantly have a reminder.
So I ask
Why do people go to war?

Emma Barker (13)
St John's School, Bishop Auckland